Cycling for Triathletes

End...

Ironman Edition

Cycling for Triathletes

I R O N M A N ®

Endurance

By Paul Van Den Bosch

Published by Meyer & Meyer Sport

Ironman and M-dot are registered trademarks of World Triathlon Corporation

British Library Cataloguing in Publication Data
A catalogue record for this book is available from the British Library

Paul Van Den Bosch
Cycling for Triathletes – Endurance
Ironman
Oxford: Meyer & Meyer Sport (UK) Ltd., 2006
ISBN 10: 1-84126-107-6
ISBN 13: 978-1-84126-107-2

© 2006 by Meyer & Meyer Sport (UK) Ltd.
Aachen, Adelaide, Auckland, Budapest, Graz, Johannesburg,
New York, Olten (CH), Oxford, Singapore, Toronto
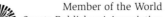 Member of the World
Sports Publishers' Association (WSPA)
www.w-s-p-a.org
Printed and bound by: B.O.S.S Druck und Medien GmbH, Germany
ISBN 10: 1-84126-107-6
ISBN 13: 978-1-84126-107-2
E-Mail: verlag@m-m-sports.com
www.m-m-sports.com

Contents

Introduction

A sport seldom experienced such a fast increase as triathlon. In only 25 years' time this complete endurance competition has evolved from a sport for eccentric people to a full-fledged Olympic discipline, getting a lot of media attention.

This evolution very quickly led to professionalism, which requires more and more of the performance level of top triathletes. This whirl of events not only pushes this last category of triathletes forward, but the subtoppers and the amateurs as well.

Does it? Are there really amateurs in triathlon? Every triathlete is driven by the unlimited ambition to always swim, run and cycle more rapidly, and everyone who finishes in an Ironman, or even a race concerning the Olympic distance, is a winner, a fully accomplished sportsman or sportswoman.

It should thus speak for itself that you need to follow specific and clear training principles and training set-ups to reach the limit of your own possibilities.

Experience teaches us that swimming and running are the two disciplines for which people train best and most efficiently. Therefore especially swimming and running coaches are the basis of the high flight that triathlon has taken in the field of performance growth.

Specific cycling training is, on the other hand, sometimes neglected by a lot of triathletes. They cycle often but in most of cases they do not go about it really professionally, and typically the main purpose of cycling training is working for the base endurance and increasing the overall weekly training volume.

However the cycling component in a race often demands more time than the two other components combined. Specific and efficient cycling training therefore could mean gaining a lot of time.

In this book I have tried to take into consideration all aspects of cycling training, which are specifically important for the triathlete. If necessary, there has been made a clearcut distinction in training for the Olympic distance and for the Ironman distance. Since drafting was allowed for the short distance races, we can indeed talk about almost two completely different cycling disciplines.

The range of items discussed is therefore very varied.

Which training forms can improve your cycling performance and how do you determine the training intensity for these training forms? Is a heart rate monitor useful? How do you spread multiple training sessions in an overall year planning, taking the nature of the race into account? What do you need to do to improve your specific strength? How do you learn to climb better? Which is the most suitable gear ratio? What influence does your body weight and your bicycle material have on your cycling performance? The answers to these questions you can find in this book, often by means of very specific examples and training set-ups.

Of course we also pay particular attention to more general issues such as overtraining. This last item must certainly not be neglected, because a lot of triathletes can easily be considered training freaks, too often underestimating the importance of recovery. Finally, nutrition and fluid intake must not be overlooked during cycling, both in a training session and during the race.

I am convinced this book will offer excellent help to triathletes of all level to trace and improve gaps in their training set-ups.

Have a lot of fun cycling!!!

Chapter 1

Various types of training

TO IMPROVE YOUR CYCLING PERFORMANCE

To improve your cycling performance during a triathlon you must, on the one hand, not only cycle frequently, but you must also add the variation necessary in your cycling training. A lot of triathletes consider their cycling training as the ideal group training session, and they too often confine themselves to just riding plenty of kilometers.

On the other hand you must also train specifically, and choose the correct priorities in function of the objectives you want to attain. If you want to finish an *Ironman distance,* you must choose other priorities during your cycling training than those preparing for an *Olympic distance.*

Energy supply of the body

To get a better idea of the different training forms available for triathletes, you need to obtain a correct insight into the energy supply of the body. We can consider the body as a constantly working engine. To keep this engine going you always need to have enough fuel. Our body needs, according the duration and the intensity of the effort, several types of fuel.

Energy for the short and intense efforts

A restricted quantity of energy has been stacked up in our body in the form of ATP (adenosine-triphosphate) and CP (creatine phosphate). This energy is immediately available, but after a few seconds, is already consumed. If the effort lasts longer than a few seconds, another energy supply must be utilized, namely glycogen. These are carbohydrates piled up in the muscles and the liver. If the effort is intense, and lasts some time, then lactic acid starts building up in the muscles. The piling-up of lactic acid presents you with a feeling of your muscles blocking, and forces you to either stop the effort, or at least dramatically scale back the intensity.

This feeling is very intense when you climb a short, steep slope at full speed, for example. After one to two minutes, not only do your legs hurt, but your arms start feeling extremely heavy. The muscles are completely full of lactic acid and it becomes impossible, in spite of all will power, to continue cycling at the same pace.

The oxidation of the above-mentioned energy sources takes place without mediation of oxygen. Therefore this is called **anaerobic energy supply.**

Energy for long-term efforts at low intensity

When the effort lasts longer, and therefore the intensity is lower as well, the body continues to appeal to multiple sources for energy. On the one hand your body continues to draw partially on the oxidation of carbohydrates, but on the other hand, and this is interesting for triathletes, also to a great extent on the oxidation of fatty acids.

The big difference from the energy supply for short-term efforts with high intensity is 1) that the amount of energy now available is much larger and therefore much slower consumed, and 2) that this kind of energy is provided with mediation of oxygen. We call this **aerobic energy supply.**

The two large energy sources are therefore fatty acids and carbohydrates. Which of these two energy sources will be utilized by the body depends in the first place on the intensity of the effort.

For a long-term effort of low intensity, energy will mainly be provided by oxidation of fatty acids. When the intensity of the effort rises, the share of carbohydrate oxidation will increase. If the carbohydrate supply is sufficient, it can provide energy for approximately 90 minutes. Its stock is therefore relatively limited. After a while the body must switch to oxidation of fatty acids.

The feeling that accompanies this change of energy supply by carbohydrates to energy supply by fatty acids is known as the infamous "punch of the hammer" or as "hitting the wall." This is caused by the fact that for the same quantity of oxygen taken in, fatty acids release less energy than carbohydrates. The moment when your carbohydrates are consumed, you suddenly obtain less energy without preceding warning. This feels like having extremely heavy legs.

This fat store in the body is seemingly inexhaustible. When a triathlete is better trained for long distances, he will still be able to utilize this fat supply for a higher intensity effort because the oxidation is more efficient than for untrained athletes. In other words, a trained triathlete can save his carbohydrate supply longer, whereas a beginner starts consuming his carbohydrates much sooner.

A good aerobic endurance capacity mainly serves efforts of relatively low intensity and considerably long duration. "Relatively" indicates that the triathlete's degree of training must be taken into account. Low intensity for a well-trained triathlete could mean high intensity for a beginner.

Conclusion:

The energy source utilized by our body during physical efforts depends on:

- The intensity of the effort
- The duration of the effort
- The situation stipulated by nutrition (extra glycogen in the body)
- The degree of training

Various types of training

Recovery training

The recovery training is carried out in order to recover from preceding training sessions. The intensity is very low, and the training volume limited. These training sessions have a favorable impact on removing the waste products in the muscles and they are generally preferred to passive recovery.

The importance of the recovery training can not be underestimated. You should train hard in order to obtain results, but the eventual training impact can be only realized during the (active) recovery period.

A real recovery training session never lasts longer than 60 to 90 minutes, depending on your degree of training. If you cycle more than 90 minutes, you cannot consider this recovery training, even for well-trained people. This should be looked upon as endurance training.

Particularly after intense running training sessions, doing recovery training on the bicycle is ideal. The movement is cyclic and not very taxing on the muscles.

Aerobic endurance training

The perfect means to improve the **aerobic endurance capacity** is aerobic endurance training. As mentioned before, this kind of endurance is *the* physical basic characteristic a triathlete should develop because it mobilizes the fat supply. Aerobic endurance training also forms the basis for all other more intensive training sessions.

The aerobic endurance capacity is often indicated by the **maximal oxygen uptake (VO_2max)**. This parameter indicates how much oxygen can be incorporated in the muscle fibers (mainly the active muscles) of the triathlete at maximum effort. VO_2max, considered absolutely, is expressed in liters per minute. Because a very muscular triathlete can take in more oxygen (considered absolutely) than a light triathlete with less muscle mass, VO_2max is divided by the weight and is expressed in ml./min/ kilogram. This is the relative capacity of oxygen uptake. High VO_2max indicates a large capacity to oxidize energy supplies (carbohydrates and fatty acids). This is of course favorable to making long-term efforts. Measuring the maximum capacity of oxygen intake is rather time-consuming, and provides no absolute value judgment concerning the aerobic capacity of the cyclist. However, it is common belief that VO_2max of 60ml/min.kg is a base requirement to achieve good results as a triathlete.

The aerobic endurance training can be subdivided into three levels:
Aerobic Endurance training level 1 (AET1), Aerobic Endurance training level 2 (AET2) and Aerobic Endurance training level 3 (AET3)

- **AET1**, also known as Long Slow Distance (LSD), is very important for a triathlete. These are training sessions which last a very long time, generally longer than a race. The pace is relatively low, so that you can easily chat during training. Energy is mainly provided by oxidation of fatty acids.

- In **AET2** as well, the training pace remains relatively low, but nevertheless higher than in the LSD. Although oxidation of fatty acids is still essential for energy supply, the share of oxidation of carbohydrates increases. This type of training prepares the triathlete for the more intensive training coming.

The AET1 and AET2 are very important because they will allow the triathlete to cycle at a higher pace on the basis of the fat metabolism, meaning cycling without the carbohydrate store being utilized.

These training forms are, of course, important for racing the *Olympic distance*. These races last about two hours, and often still a lot longer.

But these training forms count even more in the preparation for races concerning the *Ironman distance*. In this case it is essential to swim, to run and to cycle at the highest possible intensity without using too much of the carbohydrate supply.

Preparing for the *Olympic distance*, training sessions (AET1) can last two to four hours, while preparing for the *Ironman distance* these cycling training sessions can even last up to five to six hours!

HINT: Annually, spend approximately 80% of your total training volume on AET1 and AET2

- AET3 sessions are shorter than the AET1 and AET2 sessions and the intensity is significantly higher. The triathlete has a less comfortable feeling, breathing rhythm goes quicker and talking becomes more difficult.

    This training takes place in the area under the threshold (see further), and has a positive influence on the carbohydrate metabolism. By means of these high intensity endurance training sessions, the endurance limit is being moved, i.e., you can cycle at a higher speed for a longer time without lactic acid piling up.

    An AET3 on the bike generally lasts, apart from warming-up and cooling down time, 60 to maximum 120 minutes, and this prepares the triathlete for both *Olympic distance and the Ironman distance.*

As the race season approaches the AET3 sessions will gain importance. Their share should never account for more than 15 to 20% of the total training volume.

Fartlek

Fartlek, or "speed game," can be considered a form of interval training. Interval training is a training principle in which strain and recovery are systematically varied. In a speed game this alternation takes place instinctively. For example, while playing you will be taking into account the nature of the track, and build in rhythm changes during your training.

Whether the aerobic or the anaerobic endurance is being trained depends on the intensity of the high intensity segments.

HINT: Fartlek is a playful and pleasant form to train for endurance. For a triathlete, training for aerobic endurance is quintessential. Therefore you must make sure that the intensity of this training session is not too high.

Threshold training

Threshold training, or tempo endurance training sessions, are sessions carried out at the threshold, using repetitions of approximately 5 to 15 minutes. These are intensive training sessions which have a particularly favorable influence on the oxidation of carbohydrates as energy source in the body.

You should distinguish threshold training on a flat track from threshold training uphill. On a flat track, the intensity of these training sessions is just below and right on the threshold. On a hilly track, the training heart rate can be somewhat higher (therefore above the threshold) because when cycling uphill more muscle groups cooperate actively in making the effort.

Example of threshold training for a triathlete preparing for an Olympic distance:

- 15 min AET1 – 15 min AET2
- 4 to 6 times 10 min to high tempo, recovery 5 min easy riding. Make sure that the tempo is such that you can ride during the last 10 minutes still as rapidly as during the first 10 min!
- 20 to 30 min cooling down

If you prepare for an *Ironman distance* it is advisable to ride, for example, 4 to 6 x 15 min to high tempo.

Submaximal (or extensive) interval training

In submaximal (or extensive) interval training, the training load is systematically varied with (active) recuperation. The intensity of the training is above the threshold, but remains submaximal. The duration of the strain amounts to 30 seconds to 5 minutes, the number of repetitions is rather high and the recovery period between efforts is short.

These training sessions are more important for the *Olympic distance* than for the *Ironman distance.*

Example of submaximal interval training:

- 15 min AET1 – 15 min AET2
- 8 to 12 times 5 min at high tempo, recovery 2 min easy riding. Again make sure that the tempo of the last repetition is still as high as the first repetition.
- 20 to 30 min cooling down

High intensity (or intensive) interval training

High intensity interval training is the perfect means to train for **anaerobic endurance capacity**. High intensity interval training actually teaches the body to cope with this lactic acid so that its piling-up is better endured. The anaerobic endurance capacity is therefore very important for high intensity efforts of short duration.

Triathletes who prepare for the *Ironman distance* have little or no profit training for this form of endurance, especially because these training sessions, if carried out too often, have a negative impact on the aerobic endurance capacity.

Triathletes who prepare for the *Olympic distance* should integrate these training sessions from time to time into their training set-up. They should be able to react to breakaways during the cycling component. Nevertheless, for these athletes as well, it is advisable to do this kind of training only once a fortnight!

This base characteristic is best trained by doing successive short-term efforts (30 sec to 1 min 30 sec) at very high, even maximum intensity. The number of repetitions is low (3 to 5 times) and the pause between the successive efforts is incomplete, so that the lactic acid has not been removed entirely when the next effort is started upon.

These are very hard training sessions, which demand much from the triathlete. Therefore only well-trained triathletes can challenge themselves in this type of training, and moreover only on the condition that the share of these training sessions in the total training program is restricted to 2 to 5% of the total training volume.

Note: the threshold

The term threshold causes quite a lot of confusion. The term threshold implies the heart rate which borders both the aerobic energy supply level and the anaerobic energy supply level. Threshold training means training in the aerobic-anaerobic area. These training sessions are very effective to extend stamina, i.e. being able to perform without "going into the red."

Chapter 2

Determining the intensity

of the cycling training

The key to improving the performance level lies in correctly determining the training intensity paired with the type of training which you want to carry out.

In other words, if you, for instance want to carry out LSD cycling training, you must know exactly how fast (or how slow) you can cycle to realize the training impact you want from this kind of training. This type of training aims at the stimulation of oxidation of fatty acids, among other things. Too high a tempo would, however, stimulate carbohydrate oxidation.

Moreover, a correct determination of the training intensity is important to stipulate the time needed to reach supercompensation (see further).

You should not only pay attention to the quantity of training, but also to the quality (intensity) of training. This intensity can be determined under very different forms, varying from vaguely to very detailed.

You can define the quality of a cycling training session as quiet, extensive, recovery training, fartlek, intensive, etc.

You can also express the training intensity using figures, e.g. until 80% of maximum, 30 kilometers per hour, to a heart rate between 170 and 175, doing a tempo of more or less 2 mmol lactic acid.

It is obvious that, the closer the training intensity and efficiency come to overlapping, the more effective training will be.

Generally speaking the most common parameters used to define the training intensity are:
• Subjective feeling (slow, fast, quiet...)
• Heart rate frequency
• Lactic acid concentration in blood

Subjective feeling

Using this parameter you merely trust your gut instinct to determine the intensity of your cycling training. The feeling during the different training forms logically should be the following:

Recovery training and AET1 and AET2

- Comfortable
- You can still continue this tempo easily for a long time
- You breathe easily
- You can easily talk during the effort. As a matter of fact you could tell a complete story without interruptions.

AET3

- Less comfortable feeling
- Tempo is not experienced as easy, but nevertheless you can keep it up approximately 30 to 60 minutes
- You breathe more quickly and superficially
- Talking during cycling gets more difficult. Only short sentences with interruptions are still possible.

Fartlek

- The feeling during this speed game depends entirely on the quality of the intensive parts. Generally the feeling during the intensive parts is uncomfortable, and talking is difficult.

Threshold training

- Uncomfortable feeling
- You can keep up the tempo maximum 10 to 15 minutes
- You breathe rapidly and superficially
- Talking is almost impossible during this kind of training, and you must restrict yourself to pronouncing a few words

High intensity interval training

- Your legs and even your arms feel heavy and painful because of the piling-up of lactic acid in your muscles
- You breathe very quickly now
- Talking has become completely impossible, even fpr a time after finishing the effort

This subjective feeling is an important parameter. Nevertheless you must be careful with your gut instinct. If you feel good, and you are in good shape, there is a risk that the training intensity (continuously) will be too high.

Therefore it is advisable to also use other parameters to determine your optimal training intensity.

Heart rate

A commonly used method to determine the training intensity has been based on the heart rate registratered during the effort. This parameter not only provides very important information on the intensity of your training, but also on your level of condition.

It is a fact that until a certain level the heart rate increases linearly to the rising intensity of the effort, and comparing different heart rate frequencies to an equal tempo at various times gives a clear picture of the form. A better condition translates into a lower heart rate for the same effort.

In other words, if you notice that you can produce a higher tempo at a lower heart rate, this means that a positive training impact has taken place.

An improved condition is also expressed in a more rapid drop of the heart rate to rest value after the effort.

How can the heart rate be registered?

In the first place you can register the heart rate manually by feeling and counting the pulsation in the area of the heart, the carotid artery or the radial artery. This method obviously is very inaccurate, especially if the heart rate is high and you cannot count immediately after the effort.

The registration of the heart rate can be much more efficient by means of the wireless heart rate monitor. Using this heart rate monitor you remain continuously informed on your heart rate during the effort.

Training intensity based on the percentage of the maximum heart rate

You can determine your training intensity based on certain percentages of your maximum heart rate.

You can find out your maximum heart rate by cycling, after a sound warm-up of at least 10 to 15 minutes, ending with tempo accelerations of approximately one to two minutes at full speed, preferably uphill.

This maximum heart rate can be also determined during a maximum effort test at the doctor.

Sometimes the maximum heart rate is also determined by means of the rule of thumb "220-age." If you are 30 years old, you could conclude that your maximum heart rate is 190 beats per minute. Although this often meets reality, it is nevertheless best to start from your real maximum heart rate, if possible.

Remember, the maximum heart rate in itself provides absolutely no indication of your condition and is not due to your training. The maximum heart rate will gradually decrease, however, with getting older.

The heart rate areas for the different training forms can be inferred from the next table:

Nature of training	% of the maximum heart frequency
Recovery training	- 65%
AET1	66-68%
AET2	69-72%
AET3	73-82%
Threshold training on a flat track	83-86%
Threshold training uphill	87-90%
High Intensity interval training	+ 90%

This method has the advantage that it is very easily applicable.

A disadvantage, however, is that the evolution of the condition is not taken into account at all. In other words, independent of the condition, the training heart rates will always be the same since the maximum heart rate does not change due to the influence of training.

Training intensity based on the formula of Karvonen

When calculating the training intensity, the formula of Karvonen takes into account, the resting heart rate, apart from the maximum heart rate.

**% (HF maximum – HF rest) + HF rest =
HF during the effort**

For example: Your morning pulse is 50 and your maximum heart rate is 200. You want to train to 70% of the maximum intensity. The training heart rates are then calculated as follows:

0.7 (200-50) + 50 = 155

Based on the formula of Karvonen the heart rate areas for the different training forms can be calculated as follows:

Nature of training	% according to formula of Karvonen
Recovery training	60%
AET1	61-64%
AET2	65-70%
AET3	71-78%
Threshold training on a flat track	79-81%
Threshold training uphill	82-84%
Submaximal interval training	85-89%
High intensity interval training	+90%

Elaborated example: Maximum heart rate = 200
                                    Heart rate in rest = 50

- Recovery training   0.60 (200-50) + 50 = 140

- AET1   0.61 (200-50) + 50 = 141
                                  0.64 (200-50) + 50 = 146

- AET2   0.65 (200-50) + 50 = 147
                                  0.70 (200-50) + 50 = 155

- AET3   0.71 (200-50) + 50 = 156
                                  0.78 (200-50) + 50 = 167

- Threshold flat track   0.79 (200-50) + 50 = 168
                                  0.81 (200-50) + 50 = 172

- Threshold uphill   0.82 (200-50) + 50 = 173
                                  0.84 (200-50) + 50 = 176

- Submax. Interval training   0.85 (200-150) + 50 = 177
                              0.89 (200-50) + 50 = 184

- High int. Interval training   + 0.90 (200-50) + 50 = 185

The advantage of the formula of Karvonen is that this formula is well applicable to everyone. It is also a rather reliable method which shows a good correlation with the more specialized lactic acid tests.

An additional advantage is that by using this formula the condition of the triathlete is taken into account. As the resting heart rate decreases (better condition) the formula will also produce another result.

Under limit heart rate AET1 according to the formula of Karvonen

Hr/Hm	205	200	195	190	185	180	175	170
35	137	134	131	128	125	122	119	116
40	139	136	133	130	127	124	121	118
45	141	138	135	132	129	126	123	120
50	143	140	137	134	131	128	125	122
55	145	142	139	136	133	130	127	124
60	147	144	141	138	135	132	129	126
65	149	146	143	140	137	134	131	128
70	151	148	145	142	139	136	133	130
75	153	150	147	144	141	138	135	132
80	155	152	149	146	143	140	137	134

Upper limit heart rate AET1 according to the formula of Karvonen

Hr/Hm	205	200	195	190	185	180	175	170
35	144	141	137	134	131	128	125	121
40	146	142	139	136	133	130	126	123
45	147	144	141	138	135	131	128	125
50	149	146	143	140	136	133	130	127
55	151	148	145	141	138	135	132	129
60	153	150	146	143	140	137	134	130
65	155	151	148	145	142	139	135	132
70	156	153	150	147	144	140	137	134
75	158	155	152	149	145	142	139	136
80	160	157	154	150	147	144	141	138

Under limit heart rate AET2 according to the formula of Karvonen

Hr/Hm	205	200	195	190	185	180	175	170
35	144	141	137	134	131	128	125	121
40	146	142	139	136	133	130	126	123
45	147	144	141	138	135	131	128	125
50	149	146	143	140	136	133	130	127
55	151	148	145	141	138	135	132	129
60	153	150	146	143	140	137	134	130
65	155	151	148	145	142	139	135	132
70	156	153	150	147	144	140	137	134
75	158	155	152	149	145	142	139	136
80	160	157	154	150	147	144	141	138

Upper limit heart rate AET2 according to the formula of Karvonen

Hr/Hm	205	200	195	190	185	180	175	170
35	154	151	147	144	140	137	133	130
40	156	152	149	145	142	138	135	131
45	157	154	150	147	143	140	136	133
50	159	155	152	148	145	141	138	134
55	160	157	153	150	146	143	139	136
60	162	158	155	151	148	144	141	137
65	163	160	156	153	149	146	142	139
70	165	161	158	154	151	147	144	140
75	166	163	159	156	152	149	145	142
80	168	164	161	157	154	150	147	143

Under limit heart rate AET3 according to the formula of Karvonen

Hr/Hm	205	200	195	190	185	180	175	170
35	154	151	147	144	140	137	133	130
40	156	152	149	145	142	138	135	131
45	157	154	150	147	143	140	136	133
50	159	155	152	148	145	141	138	134
55	160	157	153	150	146	143	139	136
60	162	158	155	151	148	144	141	137
65	163	160	156	153	149	146	142	139
70	165	161	158	154	151	147	144	140
75	166	163	159	156	152	149	145	142
80	168	164	161	157	154	150	147	143

Upper limit heart rate AET3 according to the formula of Karvonen

Hr/Hm	205	200	195	190	185	180	175	170
35	168	164	160	156	152	148	144	140
40	169	165	161	157	153	149	145	141
45	170	166	162	158	154	150	146	143
50	171	167	163	159	155	151	148	144
55	172	168	164	160	156	153	149	145
60	173	169	165	161	158	154	150	146
65	174	170	166	163	159	155	151	147
70	175	171	168	164	160	156	152	148
75	176	173	169	165	161	157	153	149
80	178	174	170	166	162	158	154	150

Under limit heart rate "threshold training on flat road" according to the formula of Karvonen

Hr/Hm	205	200	195	190	185	180	175	170
35	168	164	160	156	152	148	144	140
40	169	165	161	157	153	149	145	141
45	170	166	162	158	154	150	146	143
50	171	167	163	159	155	151	148	144
55	172	168	164	160	156	153	149	145
60	173	169	165	161	158	154	150	146
65	174	170	166	163	159	155	151	147
70	175	171	168	164	160	156	152	148
75	176	173	169	165	161	157	153	149
80	178	174	170	166	162	158	154	150

Upper limit heart rate "threshold training on flat road" according to the formula of Karvonen

Hr/Hm	205	200	195	190	185	180	175	170
35	173	169	165	161	157	152	148	144
40	174	170	166	162	157	153	149	145
45	175	171	167	162	158	154	150	146
50	176	172	167	163	159	155	151	147
55	177	172	168	164	160	156	152	148
60	177	173	169	165	161	157	153	149
65	178	174	170	166	162	158	154	150
70	179	175	171	167	163	159	155	151
75	180	176	172	168	164	160	156	152
80	181	177	173	169	165	161	157	153

Under limit heart rate "threshold training uphill" according to the formula of Karvonen

Hr/Hm	205	200	195	190	185	180	175	170
35	173	169	165	161	157	152	148	144
40	174	170	166	162	157	153	149	145
45	175	171	167	162	158	154	150	146
50	176	172	167	163	159	155	151	147
55	177	172	168	164	160	156	152	148
60	177	173	169	165	161	157	153	149
65	178	174	170	166	162	158	154	150
70	179	175	171	167	163	159	155	151
75	180	176	172	168	164	160	156	152
80	181	177	173	169	165	161	157	153

Upper limit heart rates "threshold training uphill" according to the formula of Karvonen

Hr/Hm	205	200	195	190	185	180	175	170
35	178	174	169	165	161	157	153	148
40	179	174	170	166	162	158	153	149
45	179	175	171	167	163	158	154	150
50	180	176	172	168	163	159	155	151
55	181	177	173	168	164	160	156	152
60	182	178	173	169	165	161	157	152
65	183	178	174	170	166	162	157	153
70	183	179	175	171	167	162	158	154
75	184	180	176	172	167	163	159	155
80	185	181	177	172	168	164	160	156

Under limit heart rates "submaximal interval training" according to the formula of Karvonen

Hr/Hm	205	200	195	190	185	180	175	170
35	178	174	169	165	161	157	153	148
40	179	174	170	166	162	158	153	149
45	179	175	171	167	163	158	154	150
50	180	176	172	168	163	159	155	151
55	181	177	173	168	164	160	156	152
60	182	178	173	169	165	161	157	152
65	183	178	174	170	166	162	157	153
70	183	179	175	171	167	162	158	154
75	184	180	176	172	167	163	159	155
80	185	181	177	172	168	164	160	156

Upper limit heart rates "submaximal interval training" according to the formula of Karvonen

Hr/Hm	205	200	195	190	185	180	175	170
35	186	182	177	173	169	164	160	155
40	187	182	178	174	169	165	160	156
45	187	183	179	174	170	165	161	156
50	188	184	179	175	170	166	161	157
55	189	184	180	175	171	166	162	157
60	189	185	180	176	171	167	162	158
65	190	185	181	176	172	167	163	158
70	190	186	181	177	172	168	163	159
75	191	186	182	177	173	168	164	160
80	191	187	182	178	173	169	165	160

The registration of the resting heart rate

It is interesting to first look upon the registration and the interpretation of resting heart rate. You best register your resting heart rate lying down, some minutes after awaking. The circumstances among which the resting heart rate is registered must always be the same.

What can you infer from this?

The resting heart rate gives you an insight into the evolution of your form.

It is common practice that if your form improves, your resting heart rate decreases. On the other hand, if you train less often or not at all, after a while your resting heart rate will increase.

Your resting heart rate can be considered the barometer of the body.

An elevated resting heart rate can be a sign:
* that you have insufficiently recovered from the efforts made, either in a training session, or during a race. IF you are well trained, an increase of only some heart beats (about 5) or 10% obliges you to be careful. If you are less well trained, your resting heart rate is more liable to previous training labor. In this case your resting heart rate can be 7 to 10 beats or 15-20% higher before an alarm bell will sound.

If your resting heart rate is raised, you can best insert a rest day or a lighter training session. A further control of the resting heart rate remains necessary.

* of a viral infection such as influenza without the symptoms of the disease being already manifest. Training less or even complete rest are required to prevent that the resistance of your body against the rising infection is

undermined any further. Convalescence will go about much quicker than in case you continue to train until the syndrome manifests itself entirely.

A regular and precise registration and interpretation of the morning pulse curve can spare you a lot of inconveniences.

Notes

A low resting heart rate is no absolute value meter concerning your form. A triathlete having 45 for a resting heart rate is not necessarily in better condition than an athlete having a resting heart rate of 50. Moreover a low resting heart rate is not always a guarantee that the form is optimum (see further).

Factors influencing the heart frequency

If you use the heart rate monitor to determine your training intensity, you should also take into account a number of factors apart from cycling intensity that may influence the heart rate frequency.

Temperature and humidity degree

The heart rate increases in warm weather and high humidity, both in rest and during efforts. The heart rate reaches its most normal values between 16°C / 60°F and 20°C / 68°F.

If temperature is lower than 16°C / 60°F, it gets more difficult to reach the heart rate limits for the different types of training. As low as 12°C / 54°F, the heart rate limits can be reduced by one pulsation per degree.

Altitude

When you go on an altitude training period, you will see that your heart rate in rest and during efforts is higher than usual.

After an acclimatization period of a few days, the heart frequency in rest drops to the normal value. This also is the indicator that training can be done as usual.

However, it is much more difficult to attain the normal maximum heart rate during altitude training.

Loss of fluids

Loss of fluids increase the heart rate during effort. It is thus very important to drink sufficiently during the training sessions and the races.

Nutrition

Eating food full of carbohydrates before, and drinking energy drinks during, the training session and the race leads to a lower heart rate.

Someone who neglects to complete his carbohydrate store after high intensity training sessions and after races will no longer be able to obtain a high heart rate after a while. This will lead to being overtrained.

Refrigeration

Refrigeration during a long-term effort brings along a drop in heart frequency.

Illness

If you are ill, you have a (much) higher heart rate than usual both during rest and during effort. It cannot be stressed too often that training when you are ill is useless and even dangerous. A sick body is not trainable.

Medicines

Some medicines have a clear impact on the heart frequency.

The muscle mass used

Using more muscle mass during the effort increases the heart rate. That is why it is easier to attain a higher heart rate when cycling uphill than when cycling on a flat track.

Stress

During a race the heart rate is higher than usual especially for cyclists liable to stress. For these athletes it is thus not very useful to have a heart rate monitor during races. For these triathletes it does not make sense to register the resting heart rate on the morning of a race.

Overtraining

An athlete who is over-trained can no longer reach the maximum heart frequency. The heart rate during effort is thus lower than usual ("I cannot reach my heart rate"). Sometimes this is wrongfully interpreted as a positive sign (a lower heart rate for the same effort).

CONCLUSION

The heart rate monitor is a very useful instrument to control your training intensity. You must take into account, however, the different factors which can influence the heart frequency.

The heart rate monitor is most efficient for a triathlete during training forms in which you train to a relatively low heart rate.

Lactic acid concentration in blood

A more scientific method to determine your training intensity is determining the lactic acid concentration in your blood during an effort.

At rest the lactic acid concentration in the blood amounts to 1 to 2 mmol/liter. This lactic acid concentration remains constant as long as the triathlete remains at rest or trains to a moderate intensity. As long as the lactic acid concentration remains stable or only increases slightly, the effort can be continued for a very long time, theoretically speaking, because the lactic acid formed is being removed during the effort itself. When the effort intensity continues to increase, the lactic acid will however also start to increase in a first stage. As the intensity continues to increase, the lactic acid concentration also starts rising more dramatically, and at high intensity will eventually show a very strong increase curve. At this moment you will be obliged to stop the effort or to strongly scale back the intensity. For a well-trained triathlete the cycling speed will be higher before the curve shows a strong increase than for a less well-trained athlete.

By means of laboratory tests, a very precise link can be determined between the lactic acid concentration and the capacity of the cyclist, and between the lactic acid concentration and the heart rate.

This is generally tested using a gradual effort test on a bicycle ergometer. This means that the workload is being raised (depending on the test protocol) after a few minutes.

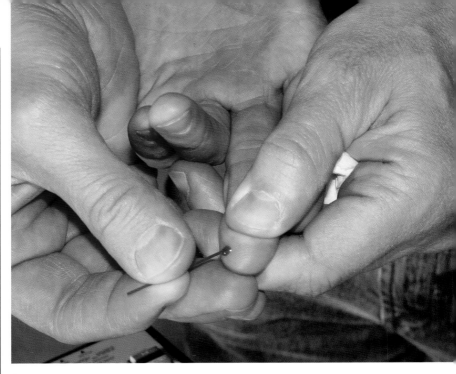

The time span of one effort stage should take at least 4 minutes because only after this period a constant lactic acid value will be reached.

The training recommendation is based on the course of the lactic acid curve. The point where the lactic acid curve shows a strong increase (heart rate 164) is vital. We can conclude that the threshold is situated here.

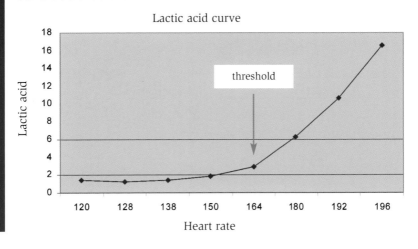

Lactic acid curve

Chapter 3

Strength training

to improve the cycling performance

Triathlon is undoubtedly a sport discipline in which a certain form of strength is significant, particularly for the cycling and swimming components Therefore it is certainly useful to spend a part of your training time during the preparation period on developing this physical basic characteristic. Furthermore we will restrict ourselves to the strength training which can improve the cycling performance.

Types of strength

To get a decent insight in the most efficient way you can carry out strength training, it is useful to take a closer look at this training component.

The strength training element can be subdivided into several components, viz. maximum strength, explosive strength and strength endurance on the one hand, and dynamic strength and static strength on the other hand.

- *Maximum strength* means the maximum resistance which can be overcome in one repetition by developing maximum muscle tension in the muscle fibers.

- *Explosive strength* is reached by the maximum muscle tension which can be developed in the muscle fibers in the shortest possible time. In other words, an external resistance must be overcome with the largest possible contraction speed.

- *Strength endurance* is defined as the capacity of repeating a relatively light strength effort during a certain time. This training element can still be differently defined as the capacity against fatigue in long-term strength efforts to a relatively low intensity in a dynamic pattern.

- *Dynamic strength training* implies that while developing muscle tension, the muscle length changes, either shortens (which is called concentric contraction), or extends (which is called excentric contraction).

- *Static strength training* means that while developing muscle, the muscle length does not change. The strength is in other words displayed in relation to a fixed resistance.

It should be clear that a triathlete especially benefits from developing strength endurance in a dynamic pattern.

Static strength training must absolutely be avoided, because the (initially fast) increase of strength rapidly stabilizes, and because the profit in muscle volume is not paired with an increase of the muscle capillarisation (capillary vessel formation around the muscles) in this form of strength training. Static muscle training is too unspecific and has a negative impact on local muscle endurance.

How does this strength training actually work?

To get more strength you can follow a general strength training program in the gym or you can carry out a strength training program on your bicycle. In principle the second, more specific method will provide the highest output.

Strength training in the gym

Strength training in the gym has several advantages. Especially if your preparation period to the triathlon season takes place in the winter, it is often more pleasant to train in the gym than to cycle outdoors in the rain and cold. Strength training in the gym is also a good supplement to your cycling training on the road.

It is very important that every triathlete gets a strength training program using a workload which has been established by means of certain individual data. This means that every strength exercise must be conducted at a percentage of the maximum workload that can be overcome by the triathlete in that specific exercise while going through the complete movement range. This maximum strain is called 1 RM, or one repetition maximum.

Determining 1RM

Determining 1RM is a very straining process because you should strive for the maximum workload for a certain exercise. Therefore you must make sure that you first do a good general warming-up (running, cycling, stepping or rowing), followed by a good specific warming-up of the muscle groups mobilized. Also make sure that you do a correct implementation of the exercises.

After a good general and specific warming-up, you should reach your maximum workload in three steps. Start at a workload which still can be overcome fairly easily. Instinctively, the load is still raised two times to the real maximum workload which can be overcome.

The correct implementation is of vital importance because during bad implementation, compensation movements are made. This means that muscle groups than those intended will be activated during the implementation of the movement. The efficiency of the strength exercise gets lost because of this, and the compensation movements often lead to overload injuries. Therefore, it is important to first learn the strength exercises guided by an expert using a light workload.

From this point of view it should be clear that working with fitness tools is preferred to strength training with weights.

Training strength endurance

If 1RM is determined for the various exercises, you should first pay attention to the improvement of **strength endurance**.

The development of strength endurance is an absolutely necessary foundation for later training of maximum strength. Strength endurance is developed by means of a large number of repetitions to 40 to 50% of 1RM. In a traditional training pattern lasting more or less eight weeks, a set-up of 30 to 100 repetitions is suggested.

To obtain optimum training impact, two to three training sessions a week are required. There must be at least one recovery day between sessions, since the muscle development during and after the training session reduces, then reaches a prime 24 to 48 hours later.

Muscles which must be trained

The different muscle groups which you must strengthen are the knee stretchers (quadriceps), the hamstrings, the buttock muscles (gluteï) and the calf muscles.

Strong quadriceps are especially important to be able to cycle powerfully. This is thus the only muscle group for which maximum strength must also be improved, in addition to the strength endurance.

Training maximum strength

After five weeks of strength endurance training you can start training for the maximum strength of the knee stretchers (quadriceps).

Training for maximum strength requires a workload of 70 to 75% of 1RM. The number of repetitions and series is lower than for the strength endurance training and the recovery period lasts longer.

A **general strength training set-up** can look like this:

week	muscle group	Repetitions	% 1RM	Recovery between series
1	all	3x10	40-50%	30"
2	all	3x12	40-50%	30"
3	all	4x10	40-50%	30"
4	all	4x12	40-50%	30"
5	• all	• 5x12	• 40-50%	• 30"
	• quadriceps	• 3x6	• 70%	• 2'-3'
6	• all	• 5x15	• 40-50%	• 30"
	• quadriceps	• 4x6	• 70%	• 2'-3'
7	• all	• 5x17	• 40-50%	• 30"
	• quadriceps	• 4x7	• 70%	• 2'-3'
8	• all	• 5x20	• 40-50%	• 30"
	• quadriceps	• 4x8	• 75%	• 2'-3'

Because of the non-specificness of the strength training in the gym, you should try to ride the ergometer bicycle 5 to 10 minutes after every leg exercise. After strength training you should cycle about half an hour on the rollers or at least one hour on the road. The objective is to transfer the strength profit obtained to the specific muscle functioning of the cycling movement.

quadriceps

calves

m. glutei

hamstrings

Specific strength training

Specific strength training means the strength training on the bicycle, cycling on an ergometer bicycle or on rollers having adjustable resistance. The greatest difficulty in this kind of specific training is finding the correct resistance.

This resistance is provided, on the one hand, by the triathlete, who is always sitting on the saddle pushing hard to make 40 to 60 rotations per minute (RPM). On the other hand you must not exceed the threshold during this training. It demands some experience and searching before specific strength training is carried out correctly.

Number of rotations per minute

Concerning the number of rotations per minute during strength training, opinions differ greatly. One point of view keeps it on 60 RPM. More rotations would hardly be called strength training, and less rotations would be too non-specific, i.e. too far remote from reality. Another point of view opts for 40 RPM, because this would allow better recovery after training.

Training set-up

This kind of training can be considerably straining for your knee tendons. That is why you should build up the training workload very gradually.

Strength training on rollers always starts with a warming-up of at least 15 minutes, in which you cycle at 100 – 120 RPM. Afterwards you cycle for a short period at a high gear ratio, 40 or 60 RPM, followed by a recovery period of a few minutes. During these recovery periods you cycle relaxed at a high pedaling frequency and at a low heart rate.

Week	Duration (minutes)	Repetitions	Recovery (minutes)
1	2	3	2
2	2	4	2
3	3	3	2
4	3	4	2
5	3	5	2
6	3	6	3
7	3	7	3
8	3	8	3
9	4	6	3

Like for strength training in the gym it is recommended to smoothly cycle 1 to 2 hours on the road with low gear ratio or 30 to 60 minutes on the rollers.

Combination strength training in the gym – specific strength training

During the preparation period you can, especially in bad weather conditions, carry out a combination of the two types of strength training.

Because the training in the gym may bring along more muscle ache than the specific strength training, it is best to let prevail the strength training in the gym on the specific strength training during the first weeks of the training set-up, in a proportion of 2 on 1. When your muscles have been adapted to the weight training, and you do not feel any muscle ache anymore, a 2-2 proportion is most suitable.

Note:

Take care when you change your bicycle, pedals and shoes. You should strive for a bicycle position as close to identical as possible to the old bicycle position. This generally is still realizable. The transfer to new shoes and pedals is far more difficult. This change must be gradual, i.e. you cannot train immediately at full strength with the new material. Possibly you should vary with the familiar material in the beginning. Especially for the specific strength training, you should be careful. To avoid injuries you must be adapted 100% to the new material before you start this kind of training.

Change of bicycle position must always be very gradual. If you decide to raise your saddle even 1 cm, this must be done progressively, each time in stages of a maximum 3 mm.

Stretching

Stretching is advisable for strength training. It is best to do stretching after a general warming-up, and not after the strength training. After the strength training the muscles must recover, and it is useless to strain them additionally with stretching exercises.

hamstrings

m. gluteï and lower back

hamstrings

ilio-tibial tract

hamstrings and adductors of the tigh

calves

Chapter 4

Time trial training

Up until about ten years ago, cycling training for triathlon only consisted of time trial training. Drafting was not allowed. Today, during Olympic distance races you can cycle in groups. But only for the Ironman distance races, the former regulation was maintained. Hence that specific time trial training will be particularly important for the long distance athletes.

Time trial is a very hard and mentally straining discipline which demands the utmost of the triathlete. You must first of all be physically strong to be able to ride such a long time trial. You must also be mentally strong to keep focused during 180 kilometers – not only on the race and your competitors, but also – and especially – on yourself. You should constantly explore your own limits, sense whether the tempo is too high, whether you can still accelerate. You must continue to ride sufficiently fast to keep your competitors in sight, or to leave them at a distance. You must also fit in spare energy at every moment, because after the cycling component there is still a long and hard marathon. Sometimes you ride a solitary race, and you cannot compare the energy level you have left to your competitors. Your only point of reference consists mainly of your own training and racing experience, which has taught you which tempo you can maintain during this long cycling component. You must also remain focused on your fluid and food intake during this component, which lasts for hours.

In short, you must be very well and specifically trained to be able to finish this component successfully, and at no time let your attention slacken.

Technical approach

During an Ironman distance, phenomenal performances are being shown during the cycling component. Take Thomas Hellriegel, for example. In 1996, during the Ironman of Hawaii, he rode an average of more than 40 kilometers per hour (4 hours 24 min and 50 sec), and this on a hilly track being always pestered by heat and wind. Jürgen Zäck, Pauli Kiuri, Mark Allen and Christian Bustos as well rode in Kona quicker than 40 kilometers per hour. This is a performance from which even a well-trained professional cyclist would back out.

The reasons for these fantastic performances are not only to be found in perfected training methods and in better medical support, but also in the evolution in material (bicycle) and the position on the bicycle.

Time trial is a technical discipline in which you must try to do all that is possible to overcome a number of opposing forces. The choice of the material, the bicycle attire and the position on the bicycle are vitally important to overcome these forces.

These opposing forces which the cyclist must overcome are: the friction caused by pedals, pedal bracket, chain and derailleur; the rolling resistance; air friction and gravity force.

The friction caused by pedals, pedal bracket, chain and derailleur

This friction is, in high-quality, well maintained bicycles, very low (5%). It is important, however, that the triathlete not let the chain of front to the back cog wheel go too slantingly. If your chain lies in front on your largest chain wheel, it is best not to use the three largest back chain wheels.

Anyhow the capacity that you produce on the pedals certainly does not completely end on the back wheel. You maximize, however, this capacity by maintaining your bicycle optimally and by high-quality bearings in all rotating elements of your bicycle.

The rolling resistance

The rolling resistance depends on a number of factors:

- *Pressure in the tires:*
    The more pressure in the tire, the less rolling resistance there will be. However a slight dent in the tire must still remain possible. On the side of the tire you can always read how much pressure can be pumped into the tires.

    Make sure that you do not put your bicycle in the sun in the transition area after having firmly pumped up the tubes. The heat will expand the air in the tires. It often happens that in the transition area the tires of bicycles that have been in the sun for quite a while explode.

- *Width of the tire:*

  Broad tires give more rolling resistance than narrow tires. On the other hand narrow tires are more vulnerable than broader ones. Only on a very smooth road without grit you can opt for very narrow tires, otherwise it is safer to choose a broader profile.

- *Diameter of the wheel:*

  The rolling resistance is inversely proportional to the diameter of the wheel. A small wheel causes more rolling resistance. This does not mean however that larger wheels have a more favorable impact than small wheels, because large wheels result in more air resistance, are heavier and block acceleration.

- *Strength exercised by the wheel on the road* (standard force).

  The rollfriction is proportional to standard force.

- *The nature of the subsoil:*

  A rough or soft subsoil causes a bigger distortion of the wheel than a hard and smooth subsoil.

Air friction

Air friction is undoubtedly the largest opposing force on flat track. On a hilly track, on the other hand, there are other and more important forces to be overcome (see further).

80 to 90% of the capacity which you must provide during the cycling component on a flat track is needed to overcome losses because of air friction.

This type of friction is far more important than roll friction, because a small change in the factors which determine air friction has a larger impact on speed than a small change in roll friction.

Air friction can be subdivided into *direct friction* and *air pressure drag.*

Direct friction arises because air layers at different speeds slide along each other and exert power on each other. The air just beside the cyclist has the speed of the cyclist. Further from the cyclist there are air layers with another speed. This way air layers arise which pass each other at different speeds.

A disk wheel causes less air friction than a normal spoke wheel. Using a normal spoke wheel a bunch of small vortexes arise when rotating, and this causes restraint. A disk wheel on the other hand causes much less turbulence, and less restraint arises.

Because a disk wheel is not always as useful in windy conditions (influence of the side wind onto the wheel), you can also opt for a wheel having three or four spokes. Even in this case there is significantly less turbulence than for a traditional wheel, and you feel the disadvantage of side wind less.

Air pressure drag is the most important form of air friction.

This friction arises because the air in front of the cyclist is slightly pressed, whereas the air behind the cyclist is sucked away (slipstream). The small difference in pressure which arises in front of and behind the cyclist causes an opposing force. This difference in pressure also brings about the so-called slipstream behind the cyclist. Riding in this slipstream is very efficient because the air pressure there is lower and because the air already has a forward speed. Riding behind someone else requires 33% less capacity than riding upfront. Riding in pairs can raise the speed by 5%, riding with 4 to 6 people can mean a profit in speed of 10%.

These data show to that energy used during a race in which drafting has been allowed strongly differs from the energy used during the cycling component of an Ironman distance, and that the strict application of the "no drafting" regulation is very important in the latter case.

The resistance depends on the perpendicular diameter of the frontal surface, on the streamline, on the smoothness of the surface and on the air density.

The *frontal surface* is the visible surface of the front of the cyclist and the bicycle. This surface can strongly be influenced by the cyclist by adopting a position bending forward. Solidly built triathletes can, on the one hand, display much strength during a time trial, but they have, on the other hand, a disadvantage because their frontal surface is too large.

The *streamline* is the measure which indicates to what extent air can gradually flow along the cyclist and the bicycle without having to make too many abrupt deviations. The streamline can be influenced among other things by cycling with oval frame tubes.

It is however still more important that you seek the ideal streamline yourself by, for instance, wearing an aerodynamic helmet. Remember, 75% of the friction is exercised on the cyclist and only 25% on the bicycle.

A *smooth surface* also reduces the air friction. That is why you profit from a tight-fitting, smooth triathlon suit or tank top during a race.

Finally air friction is proportional to *air density*.

Air density directly coincides with atmospheric pressure. The lower the pressure, the less air friction. A low atmospheric pressure can arise in two ways: by drops in pressure as a result of depressions, and as a result of the decrease in pressure at increasing altitude above sea level.

At high altitudes you should thus be able to ride more quickly. This is not the case, because thin air causes a lack of oxygen. This is particularly important for long-term efforts.

The anticipation of all these factors is very important and can mean a serious gain in time during the cycling component of a triathlon.

You should also take into account that by raising the speed, the increase in air friction is quadratic. This implies that as the triathlete cycles more rapidly he should provide a relatively greater capacity. As a rule of thumb one can state that you will have to provide 3% more capacity for 1% higher speed.

Gravity force

This opposing force is directly paired with the influence of weight on the cycling speed.

The weight of the cyclist influences the friction to be overcome in two ways. The rolling resistance is proportional to the total weight of the triathlete and the bicycle, and the weight of the triathlete influences air friction because a heavy triathlete generally also has a larger perpendicular diameter and therefore more air friction must be conquered.

The weight of the bicycle in itself is of relatively little importance, because the rolling resistance on the road is rather small. The largest part of the roll friction is caused by the body weight of the triathlete.

On flat track this is of little or no importance because heavier triathletes neutralize larger friction losses by a higher capacity.

On hilly roads, on the other hand, weight is far more important, because here the influence of gravityation is signaling higher.

On a slope of 10%, reaching a speed of 16 km/hours, only 5% of opposing force is provided by air friction and 90% by gravity.

From a slope steeper than 5% onwards, the capacity that needs to be provided at a certain speed is approximately proportional to the weight of the triathlete. A triathlete who is 10% heavier must provide approximately 8.5% more capacity. This 8.5% is not completely counterbalanced by the larger capacity that a more muscular triathlete may provide over a light triathlete. Hence, light triathletes are always favored when climbing.

Technical tips for races in which drafting is not allowed

- Adjust the position on the bicycle so that the frontal surface becomes as small as possible. This can be done by bending the torso forward, keeping the head as much as possible down during the time trial, keeping the elbows near each other. This certainly gets easier when using triathlon bars. Of course you have to find a balance between a good aerodynamic position and a position you can maintain rather comfortably during several hours.

  This requires long training sessions in which race conditions are being simulated and in which this aerodynamic position is trained to race speed. You must not forget that after finishing the cycling component you have to start a marathon. You can therefore not afford to get a back ache during cycling.

- Wear a tight-fitting triathlon suit or tank top.

- Wear a helmet in aerodynamic form.

- Ride with narrow, firmly pumped tires. When choosing tires take the nature of the road surface into account.

- Ride using a disk wheel if there is little wind and on a flat track. In case of wind and time trials including climbing, three or four spoke wheels should be preferred to disk wheels.

- Ride a light bicycle with flat, oval tubes.

Note:

Fluid intake is very important during a triathlon, especially at the *Ironman distance*. You must take along sufficient stock. Beside two drinking bottles (75 cl) which can be taken along in the holders assembled to the framework, often two additional drinking bottles are still taken along in a holder attached behind the saddle.

You must, however, take into account that, certainly on a hilly track, these bottles bring along an extra weight of 3 kilograms, and that particularly the bottles behind the saddle strongly disturb the ideal streamline. If possible, depending on the provision posts available, it would be best to confine yourself to 2 bottles which can be taken along in the traditional holders.

Choose the correct gear ratio

If you want to ride rapidly in a time trial, meaning the cycling part of an *Ironman distance*, it is important to get to a high gear ratio smoothly turning. This requires a combination of strength and suppleness.

How **specific strength** can be improved has been discussed earlier on. This strength training is preferably done during the preparation period. The impact reached then will be maintained later on in the season, doing this specific strength training once again and doing regular training sessions uphill using a high gear ratio.

It is also advisable to pay some attention to suppleness during a race. You choose your gear ratio in such a way that you can cycle to a relatively high pedaling frequency;  this means at least 90 RPM, preferably 100 RPM or more. The advantage of a high pedaling frequency is that you rather charge your cardio-vascular system, and you spare your leg muscles. This is favorable to be able to start running with fit legs. To spare your leg muscles during the race you can cycle to a low gear ratio, especially during the last part of the cycling component,. This way you prepare optimally for the running component.

Professional cyclists also do their time trials with a high pedaling frequency. During attempts to improve the hour record they generally cycle to 100 to 105 RPM. At time trials on the road they also ride to a high pedaling frequency.

How can suppleness be trained?

Training on rollers

Suppleness training on rollers is preferably done on fixed rollers having adjustable resistance; this means that the bicycle is attached onto the roller system. This allows safe cycling with a very high pedaling frequency.

This system is really preferable to the stationary bike, because it is very important that you adopt your normal cycling position during this training.

It is useful to assemble a pedaling frequency meter onto your bicycle, so that you always have an exact idea of your pedaling frequency.

You should learn to cycle with a high pedaling frequency without "shocking" on your bicycle. During these training sessions make sure that you continue to sit firmly on the saddle and that your torso moves as little as possible.

During training you progressively force up the number of rotations, until you reach the level you can handle without shocking on your saddle.

The resistance of the roller system remains low. The aim of this kind of training is certainly not anaerobic training. Thanks to the low resistance of the roller system you can, and must, be able to keep your heart rate under the threshold pulse, in spite of a very high pedaling frequency.

Example of suppleness training on rollers:

Warming up	• 10 to 15 min with low resistance, 90 rpm	• Level AET1
Main	• 3 min, 100 rpm	• Level AET2
	• 2 min, 90 rpm	• Level AET1
	• 3 min, 105 rpm	• Level AET2
	• 2 min, 100 rpm	• Level AET1
	• 3 min, 110 rpm	• Level AET2
	• 2 min, 100 rpm	• Level AET1
	• 3 min, 115 rpm	• Level AET3
	• 2 min, 100 rpm	• Level AET1
	• 3 min, 120 rpm	• Level AET3
	• 2 min, 100 rpm	• Level AET1
	• 3 min, + 120 rpm	• Level AET3
Cooling down	• 10 to 15 min, 90-100 rpm	• Level AET1

The progression in this kind of training can consist of you forcing up the number of minutes that you ride with a high pedaling frequency, and of you carrying out several sessions in which you reach a pedaling frequency of more than 120 rpm.

These training sessions are already carried out at the beginning of the preparation period, one to two times per week. Afterwards, and even during the race period, these training sessions get a spot within the training set-up.

Cycling with a fixed gear

Cycling with a fixed gear is a kind of training which is not commonly used among triathletes.

It is a kind of training especially applied to Italian professional cyclists, but it isalso useful for triathletes.

This is a type of training that is also best done during the preparation period. At a first stage you cycle with a low gear ratio, for example 39x17. As the preparation period progresses you can ride gradually with a higher gear ratio, but you must ensure that you can always continue to do at least 100 rpm. You can even train on a hilly track with a fixed gear. The training scope is forced up from 1 hour to even 3 hours (at a later stage of the preparation period). You do this one to two times per week.

Which are the advantages of such training sessions?

First of all it is an excellent way to train suppleness. You continuously do 100 rpm, often even more.

Secondly the output of these training sessions is much higher. You pedal constantly, which means the training heart rate can be kept at an even level.

Training with a fixed gear can be dangerous and demands great concentration. Doing curves involves a certain risk, and stopping suddenly is not always easy. For this reason you will best do this kind of training on quiet roads.

Example of strength and suppleness training during the first two weeks of the preparation period.

The beginning of the preparation period generally means early November. In Europe the weather conditions are not always encouraging to go and cycle outdoors. It is useful to do a cycling training session on rollers emphasizing strength, varied with suppleness.

Week 1

Day	Type	Description
Monday	Strength training	Specific strength training on the rollers Core: 3 x 2 min high resistance, 40-60 rpm
Tuesday	AET1-2 Suppleness	60 min fixed gear 39 x 17
Wednesday		
Thursday	Strength training	Specific strength training on the rollers Core: 3 x 2 min high resistance, 40-60 rpm
Friday		
Saturday	Suppleness	60 min suppleness training on the rollers
Sunday		Recovery day

Week 2

Day	Type	Description
Monday	Strength training	Specific strength training on the rollers Core: 4 x 2 min high resistance, 40-60 rpm
Tuesday	AET1-2 Suppleness	75 min fixed gear 39 x 17
Wednesday		
Thursday	Strength training	Specific strength training on the rollers Core: 4 x 2 min high resistance, 40-60 rpm
Friday		
Saturday	Suppleness	60 min suppleness training on the rollers
Sunday		Recovery day

Cycling training behind the motorcycle

Training sessions behind the motorcycle are particularly efficient to force up your cycling tempo for the 180 kilometers cycling component.

We distinguish specific tempo training behind the motorcycle, from training behind the motorcycle which has been incorporated in a long cycling training session.

Specific tempo training behind the motorcycle

The complete training session is preferably done behind the motorcycle. Since the intensity of this kind of training session is high, there must be enough attention to warming up. This warming-up lasts approximately 30 minutes. During the second part of this warming up, short rhythm changes are performed without you being out of breath. At the end of these tempo changes you can ride along with the motorcycle for a while, not too long however to prevent lactic acid from piling up in the muscles. Afterwards you still ride another ten minutes at low intensity.

Afterwards a number of block-systems follow: a number of repetitions are done to high intensity (race tempo or even somewhat higher), in which you will be riding 10 to 15 meters behind the motorcycle, or beside the motorcycle. The tempo during the block-systems is therefore maximal, but you must of course be able to ride just as fast during the last repetition (block-system) as during the first block. You ride to "maximum lactate steady state" (MLSS); this is the tempo which can still be maintained during the effort without lactic acid increasing. This point is very individualized, but one could state that this point on average lies between 4 and 6 mmol lactic acid. It has been proven to be very difficult to stipulate this point by experiment. That is why it is better to use your instincts, and to take into account that the tempo must be kept the same during every block-system.

The number of repetitions and the length of time of the block-systems depend on the duration of the race for which you prepare. When involving an *Ironman distance* the duration of a block-system will be 15 minutes.

Secondly your conditional readiness is also important. In principle you only do these training sessions when you have a very good basic condition. The number of repetitions then varies from 3 to 6. In between the block-systems you recuperate by continuing to ride to the same tempo, but now directly in the wheel of the motorcycle. You always strive for at least 100 rpm.

Such training sessions are best carried out with your racing bicycle, so that the material can be tested and so that you canalso train in your aerodynamic position.

If you prepare for the *Olympic distance*, you can also complete this kind of training entirely right behind the motorcycle, riding alternately to a very high tempo and to a lower tempo by way of recovery behind the motorcycle. You do not train however with triathlon handlebars, but with ordinary handlebars. This kind of training aims at the ability to ride at high tempo in a pack.

These training sessions are very demanding of you. . Make sure that you do a good easy ride after such a training session and that you plan a recovery day in your training set-up.

Tempo training behind the motorcycle during a long duration training

A particularly good way of training to prepare for the "long distance triathlon" consists of doing the second part of a very long cycling training session behind the motorcycle.

For example

- Total: 220 kilometers
- Part 1: 120 kilometers by yourself, level AET1 – AET2, always suppleness
- Part 2: 100 kilometers behind the motorcycle, level AET2, always suppleness

There are a variety of advantages to this kind of training:

- You keep your tempo high. You often tend to drop the tempo to the end of a long training.

- Your heart rate remains at a constant level, or is even a little bit higher during the second part of the training session.

- You bring variation into your long cycling training sessions, which can sometimes become monotonous.

- You get used to a high tempo without your training heart rate being too high.

- Finally you can continue to emphasize suppleness till the end of your training.

Chapter 5

Climbing training

A triathlete is often faced with a race course that involves quite a lot of climbing during the cycling component. The slopes vary from short and very steep, to longer and less steep. The track of the Olympic Games in Athens was, for example, one in which climbers were really favored.

For some athletes, such races are a blessing, because they can take some distance from a number of better runners. Large gaps can be created during the cycling component, and you can start the running component with a drastically thinned out group. Athletes who have no climbing capacities at all have, on such tracks, already completely lost in advance.

If you want to become a competitive triathlete, it is necessary to fully develop your climbing capacities.

Climbing training sessions can be done on roller systems with an adjustable electromagnetic resistance and on the road. Although it is more interesting to train specifically on the road, rollers offer a good alternative when weather conditions do not allow training on a hilly track.

Climbing training on rollers

Most of the current roller systems allow programming a slope percentage. The great difference with strength training on rollers is in the difference in intensity and in pedaling frequency. Whereas in strength training the heart rate remains relatively low (under threshold) and the pedaling frequency amounts to around 40 to 60 RPM, climbing training means training to a higher heart rate and to at least 80 RPM.

Climbing training is only started upon when the base endurance is satisfactory. The intensity in the first training sessions is still relatively low (up to some maximum beats above threshold).

Progression in this kind of training involves extending the training duration, raising the training intensity (cycling to a higher heart rate) and riding at higher gear ratio. Nevertheless you should always strive for suppleness when training.

During the preparation period it is advisable to train at or just beyond the threshold. For more intensive training sessions, climbing training on the road is more suitable. Due to the monotony of roller training the duration remains limited.

Example of a climbing training session on rollers:

To be able to do a decent climbing training on rollers you need to be equipped with a roller system which allows programming your slope percentages

- 15 min warm-up, more than 100 RPM
- instinctively accelerating a few times without really being out of breath
- 4 repetitions of 5 to 10 min (based on your fitness level In between the repetitions always 5 min easy riding, more than 100 RPM
  - 1°: slope percentage 6%,
    - more than 80 RPM
    - heart rate at threshold
  - 2°: slope percentage 8%,
    - more than 80 RPM
    - heart rate some beats above threshold
  - 3°: slope percentage 6%,
    - more than 80 RPM
    - heart rate at threshold
  - 4°: slope percentage 10%
    - more than 80 RPM
    - heart rate some beats above threshold,
    - alternating 2 min seated – 2 minutes out-the saddle
- 15 min easy riding, more than 100 RPM

Climbing training on the road

Climbing training on the road is of course preferable to climbing training on rollers. It is ideal to go on a training trip abroad, where long slopes can be found.

For climbing training you need slopes that last at least 10 to 15 minutes. Climbing training sessions must be built up gradually. In a first stage you should cycle uphill to a heart rate at the threshold. The further progression of climbing training depends on the fact if you prepare for a race involving the long distance or the Olympic distance.

Climbing training for Olympic distance races

The intensity during these races can be very high, and there can be drastic rhythm changes when cycling uphill. Often the slopes are used to take some distance from the less accomplished cyclists.

You therefore must be able to react to these rhythm changes or carry them out. You will have to prepare for lactic acid piling up in your muscles. As a result, the intensity of your climbing training must be very high from time to time.

In a short dicstance race , you seldom need to climb a really long slope. In this case you do not need to go and look for real mountains for your training. Slopes lasting a few kilometers, which take you a maximum 10 to 15 minutes to climb to the top, are more than enough for this kind of training.

Climbing training during the preparation period

Training 1

- 30 min warm-up, low gear ratio, doing some instinctive rhythm changes

- 4 times a slope of approximately 10 min
  - 1° and 3° repetition some beats under threshold, minimum 80 rpm
  - 2° and 4° repetition at threshold, minimum 80 rpm

- 30 min cooling down, minimum 100 rpm

- In between the slopes approximately 5 min recovery

Training 2

- 30 min warm-up, low gear ratio, doing some instinctive rhythm changes

- 5 times a slope of approximately 10 min
  - 1° and 3° repetition some beats under threshold, minimum 80 rpm
  - 2° and 4° repetition at threshold, minimum 80 rpm
  - 5° repetition about five beats above the threshold, minimum 80 rpm

- 30 min cooling down, minimum 100 rpm

- In between the slopes approximately 5 min recovery

Training 3

- 30 min warm-up, low gear ratio, doing some instinctive rhythm changes

- 6 times a slope of approximately 10 min
  - 1°, 3° and 5° repetition some beats under threshold, minimum 80 rpm
  - 2° and 4° repetition at threshold, minimum 80 rpm
  - 6° repetition about five beats above the threshold, minimum 80 rpm

- 30 min cooling down, minimum 100 rpm

- In between the slopes approximately 5 min recovery

Climbing training during the specific period

Training 1

- 30 min warm-up, low gear ratio, doing some instinctive rhythm changes
- 6 times a slope of approximately 10 min
  - 1° repetition: some beats under threshold, minimum 80 rpm
  - 2° repetition: at threshold, minimum 80 rpm
  - 3° repetition: some beats above threshold, last min at full speed, minimum 80 rpm
  - 4° repetition: suppleness, low heart rate, minimum 80 rpm
  - 5° repetition: some beats above threshold, minimum 80 rpm
  - 6° repetition: 8 min some beats above threshold, last 2 min at full speed, minimum 80 rpm
- 30 min cooling down, minimum 100 rpm
- In between the slopes approximately 5 min recovery

Training 2

- 30 min warm-up, low gear ratio, doing some instinctive rhythm changes
- 6 times a slope of approximately 10 min
  - 1° repetition: some beats under threshold, minimum 80 rpm
  - 2° repetition: some beats above threshold, minimum 80 rpm
  - 3° repetition: some beats above threshold, last 2 min at full speed, minimum 80 rpm
  - 4° repetition: suppleness, low heart rate, minimum 80 rpm

- 5° repetition: some beats above threshold, alternating 2 min out-the saddle, 2 min seated, minimum 80 rpm
- 6° repetition: 5 min some beats above threshold, last 5 min at full speed, out-the saddle, minimum 80 rpm
- 30 min cooling down, minimum 100 rpm
- In between the slopes approximately 5 min recovery

The point of these training sessions is that you really seek a rhythm to ride uphill, and that you also train yourself mentally to learn to maintain this rhythm.

There are also races in which you need to climb rather short, but steep slopes several times. In this case triathletes often make the mistake of wanting to ride uphill at too high a gear ratio. During training on similar slopes look for a gear ratio that suits you best. Take into account that the separation from the other athletes is actually earned shortly after the slope. During climbing most of the athletes are well matched. The athlete who can change to a higher gear ratio when the slope "drops," and can continue immediately to high tempo, generally makes the difference. Make sure to train this ability.

Climbing training for Ironman distance races

When you prepare for climbing during Ironman distance races, you must keep in mind that you must prepare for climbing to an even tempo which you can continue for a long time. The aim of these training sessions is to learn to ride uphill for a long time to as fast a tempo as possible without lactic acid piling up. In other words it does not make sense to train to a very high intensity with drastic rhythm changes. As a matter of fact it is useless to cycle to too high intensity uphill. Cycling uphill is merciless, and it immediately has an enormous impact on your body. Your breathing and heart rhythm immediately react to the smallest slope percentage. Your muscles are right away and continuously strained because when cycling uphill real recovery is excluded. If you have cycled and exceeded your capacities, it is even hard to cycle to a slower tempo afterwards.

For this reason it is strongly advisable to do most training sessions at the threshold, and this way try and get the cycling tempo at the threshold as high as possible.

Training 1
- 60 min warm-up, low gear ratio, using some instinctive rhythm changes
- 6 times a slope of approximately 15 min
  - 1° repetition: some beats under the threshold, minimum 80 rpm
  - 2° repetition: at the threshold, minimum 80 rpm
  - 3° repetition: some beats above the threshold, minimum 80 rpm
  - 4° repetition: very quiet tempo (try to recover), minimum 80 rpm
  - 5° repetition: some beats under the threshold, minimum 80 rpm

- 6° repetition: as fast as possible, but always even tempo, minimum 80 rpm
- 60 min easy endurance training, suppleness, more than 100 rpm.
- In between the repetitions 5 min recovery

Note

The highest possible tempo is required during the 6° repetition. This is so because at that moment little or no piling-up of lactic acid will take place due to fatigue.

Training 2

When you prepare for a race in which a real mountain must be climbed, you best train with repetitions (2) of 30 minutes. You must go and find a really mountainous track for this kind of training.

- 60 min warm-up, low gear ratio, using some instinctive rhythm changes
- 2 times a slope of approximately 30 min,
  - 1° repetition: 15 min some beats under the threshold – 15 min at the threshold, minimum 80 rpm
  - 2° repetition: 15 min at the threshold – 15 min some beats above the threshold, minimum 80 rpm. During this 2° repetition you can regularly cycle out ofthe saddle
- 60 min easy endurance training, suppleness, more than 100 rpm.
- In between the repetitions 15 min recovery

The role of weight in climbing capacity

In contrast to cycling on a flat track, weight influences performance a lot in climbing. The reason for this can be found in the fact that during climbing gravity is the largest opposing force that needs to be overcome.

The table below illustrates the decisive role of weight loss for climbing performances:

Reference point is a triathlete weighing 75 kilograms and being 5 kilograms overweight (ideal weight is thus 70kg). This cyclist provides a capacity of 300 Watts on an 8% slope.

Time profit of weight loss

Distance	Weight loss	- 1 kg	- 2 kgs	- 3 kgs	- 4 kgs	- 5 kgs
5 km		13 sec	25 sec	38 sec	51 sec	1min 5 sec
8 km		20 sec	39 sec	1 min	1 min 21 sec	1 min 40 sec
10 km		25 sec	51 sec	1 min 14 sec	1 min 39 sec	2 min 5 sec
15 km		38 sec	76 sec	1 min 54 sec	2 min 29 sec	3 min 10 sec

If you want to perform in a race involving climbing, it is therefore important to be "sharp." Weight loss must however occur gradually, and can never adopt absurd proportions. You must always take your constitution into account. Too much weight loss inevitably leads to strength loss and, within a rather short period, to overtraining (see further). If you want to lose weight you cannot economize on your carbohydrate intake during and after training sessions.

It should also be clear that not only your own weight is important for your climbing capacity, but the weight of your bicycle as well. Therefore you should choose light material.

Chapter 6

Cycling training

of a triathlete within the overall training set-up

Your cycling training sessions are difficult to separate from your running and swimming training sessions. During the year you do not need to always train in the same way and the same intensity, nor pay as much attention to different disciplines.

To get a good insight in this matter, we should first discuss the general principles of a training set-up, and examine how your cycling training fits in.

A (training) year is divided into a number of periods, and you need to plan the training sessions and races as a function of the goalsyou want to reach during these different periods. This planning can also include several years.

In this planning, several factors are of importance, such as top races, competition races, student holidays and examination periods, the strengths and weaknesses of the triathletes, injury sensitivity, weather conditions,....

This training planning can be spread out over:
- several years: long-range plan
- 1 year: macrocycle or year planning
- 4-8 weeks: mesocycle
- 1-3 weeks: micro-cycle

Long-range plan

When you notice that your cycling component is weak, you must consider the option to pay less attention to the running and swimming component, and especially pay attention to your cycling training during a complete year. This can be in the longer term a profitable vision. Once you have reached a certain level for your weaker component, you can then pay more attention to other disciplines, while maintaining your improved cycling level.

Year planning

Generally speaking, a one-year plan is subdivided into a preparation period, a specific period, a race period and relative recovery period.

The preparation period

Not taking into account a few exceptions, most important triathlons are situated in the period from May to late-

September/mid-October (Ironman in Hawaii). The preparation period therefore generally starts end November and lasts to the end of March.

You need a recovery period of at least 4 weeks, because you must be not only physically, but also mentally, recharged to start upon a new training set-up.

First of all, a thorough medical check-up is essential. You must be certain that your blood values are again at a considerable level, and that no traces of the heavy physical efforts made are detected.

The objectives for the next race season are fixed and these will, to a great extent, determine the rhythm of the training set-up. Roughly speaking, you plan during this period a gradual advancement from quiet (extensive) training sessions to more intensive training sessions. The intensive training sessions increase as the race season approaches.

Nevertheless, rather early in the preparation period, you can already do some more intensive training sessions with stimulation of the anaerobic capacity.

The advantages of this approach are:
- You strain the different energy supply systems. The variation in training ensures that both the fat metabolism and the carbohydrate metabolism are stimulated.
- There is a positive influence on the oxygen intake capacity The maximum oxygen intake capacity is not only improved by slow duration training sessions, but also by training sessions involving the aerobic-anaerobic range.
- You avoid monotony, thereby reducing the risk of overtraining.

- You have less chance of reaching performance level stagnation. Performance improvement is only possible when you train in a varied way.

Nevertheless the training volume during this period generally keeps prevailing on the intensity of the training sessions. In the beginning of the preparation period you must pay close attention to the development of aerobic endurance. Therefore the long, easy endurance training sessions remain by far the most important type of training.

This does not mean that these training sessions must be monotonous. You can, for instance, at the beginning of a long cycling training session, after the warm-up phase, do some short, submaximal rhythm changes.

Especially at the beginning of the preparation period, cycling training does not yet really get much consideration, because for a lot of triathletes the weather conditions in the winter often do not allow long cycling training sessions, and because you can build up your cycling condition in a shorter time period than your swimming and running level. Therefore, first of all, take into account these latter disciplines.

Training sessions on rollers are very interesting during this period, especially the strength training sessions which provide a very high output, in spite of the restricted training time spent.

This does not mean of course that you cannot cycle on the road during your preparation period. But force up longer endurance training sessions only towards the end of the preparation period.

In practice this means the cycling training sessions during the preparation period:

December
- 2 times strength training on rollers
- 1 time an easy endurance training on the road of approximately 2 to 3 hours. This training can also be replaced by suppleness training on rollers.

January and February
- 2 times strength training on rollers. 1 strength training can be replaced by climbing training on rollers.
- 1 to 2 times an easy endurance training on the road of approximately 2 to 3 hours.
- 1 suppleness training on rollers.

March
- 1 time strength training on rollers
- 1 time climbing training on rollers
- 1 time an easy endurance training on the road of 2 to 3 hours
- 1 time an easy endurance training on the road of 3 to 4 hours.

The specific period

During the preparation period the foundation was made for race-specific training sessions. From now on you will train harder and more specifically.

It is also best to only train on the road, although training sessions on rollers are still taken into consideration sporadically when the conditions do not allow cycling outdoors at all, or when you can only spend a limited time on your cycling training.

Preparation for the Olympic distance

During the specific period, the training intensity increases strongly, especially for those who prepare for *Olympic distance* races.

You do this by threshold training sessions, in which you cycle during approximately 10 minutes at the threshold, both on flat track and uphill.

For example:
* 30 min warm-up, instinctively some tempo changes
* 4 to 6 time 10 min at threshold, + 90 RPM, recovery 3 to 5 min suppleness, + 100 RPM
* 20 to 30 min easy riding, + 100 RPM

Besides this kind of training, you can also carry out some training sessions in group, in which you cycle to high tempo and you take alternatively the head position. You can carry out a few breakaways, and try to cycle in front of the group for a while.

These training sessions are, however, very intensive.

Because training sessions with a higher intensity rather rapidly have a negative influence on basic endurance, you must ensure that the easy endurance training sessions are still taken sufficiently into consideration in the total training volume, even if you are preparing for the short race distances.

During this period you can, by way of training, participate in some smaller races to acquire race rhythm and to get a good insight in your possible shortcomings.

Preparation for the Ironman distance

If you prepare for the Ironman distance it is now time to integrate really long endurance training sessions (5 hours and longer), including training sessions which must make sure that your race tempo gets higher. The latter is best accomplished by means of threshold training sessions.

- The long endurance training sessions -

    These training sessions are very important when preparing for the long distance. You learn to cycle at a higher tempo on the basis of the oxidation of your fatty acids.

    The tempo is relatively low, but try towards the end of the training session to continue to ride to the same tempo, and make sure your heart rate remains just as high. If you are fatigued, you will see that it becomes more and more difficult to continue to ride at the same heart rate during the last part of the training.

    You can also do this by completing the second part of the training session behind the motorcycle. This kind of training is best done once a week.

- The threshold training sessions-

    You do these sessions in the same way as when preparing the Olympic distance. You , however, force up the total volume of this training by letting the warm-up and cool down last longer. Essential in this kind of training is not the total volume, but riding to a high tempo during the specific tempo training.

    This kind of training demands much from your body. Restrict yourself to one training session per week, certainly if you take into account the intensive training sessions which are undoubtedly carried out for the other two disciplines.

TIP: Forcing up the training intensity also means that you must pay enough attention to the recovery phase.

The race period

This is a very difficult period because you must find a balance between races, recovery, specific race training and basic training. Lacking the latter makes it so difficult to keep a peak condition for a longer time. Therefore it is necessary to regularly plan a break in racing so you can spend sufficient time on recovery and basic training.

Whether or not you still carry out cycling training sessions during a period with successive races, depends on your training for other disciplines. If you still train intensively for swimming and/or running, the cycling training sessions are especially useful as recovery training or as training for basis endurance.

The relative recovery period

After a race period you are tired, both mentally and physically. A complete stop in training for one to two weeks is generally enough to recover. After this training stop you can best resume exercise sports, preferably by means of alternative practices such as swimming, cycling, playing tennis etc. The aim for this period is not raising the specific performance possibilities, but maintaining a certain fitness level as a basis for the coming preparation period.

The relative recovery period generally lasts four to six weeks.

The mesocycles

After you have planned your training roughly for the whole year, you must plan further, considering periods of four to eight weeks. This period is called a mesocycle. The basic forms of the mesocycles are the standard cycle, the increasing and decreasing block-system cycle, and the thrust cycle.

The standard cycle

standard cycle

weeks

Properties
- A gradual and progressive increase of the training volume;

- An increase in training volume of approximately 15% per week to prevent overload;

- Suitable for forcing up the training quantity;

- The standard cycle is particularly used at the beginning of the preparation period or after a period of inactivity;

- Be careful of overload because there is no room left for recovery periods.

The increasing block-system cycle

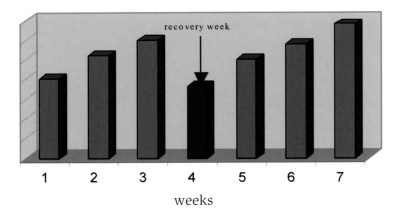

Increasing block-system cycle

recovery week

weeks

Properties

- The increase of the training volume goes in a wave-like motion;

- Suitable for forcing up the training quantity;

- The increasing block-system cycle is particularly used during the second part of the preparation period;

- A test can be carried out at the end of the fourth week;

- Week 1 < week 5, week 2 < week 6, week 3 < week 7

- Week 3 and week 7 are weeks with a high training volume. These weeks are very suitable for planning a large training volume of cycling.

The decreasing block-system cycle

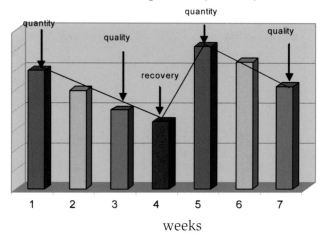

decreasing block-system cycle

Properties

- The training set-up goes in a wave-like motion;

- Suitable for forcing up training quality: if the volume decreases the training intensity can increase;

- The decreasing block-system cycle is especially used during the specific period;

- Tests are easily fit in (after some recovery days during the recovery week);

- Risk of overload in the fourth week because there is large difference between week four and week five.

- Week 5 > week 1, week 6 > week 2, week 7 > week 3

- Weeks 1 and 5 are especially suitable for a large training volume of cycling. During week 2 and 6 the emphasis is preferably on raised training intensity for swimming and running. During weeks 3 and 7 you can plan more intensive cycling training sessions.

The thrust cycle

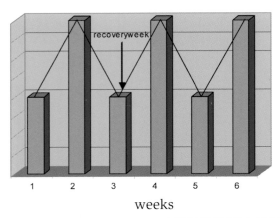

thrust cycle

weeks

Properties

- Alternate between high and low strain;

- The thrust cycle is especially suitable for the race period (peaks);

- Risk of overload because of the large volume differences;

- The thrust cycle is only suitable for very well trained athletes who have a very good basic condition.

The microcycle (week cycle)

In a week cycle as well, a wave-like motion should be observed in the intensity. You would rather not train intensively two days in a row. An intensive training day is followed by a training day in which you train to a more moderate intensity. Afterwards a relatively light training day follows.

Example of a one week plan

In the scheme mentioned below, the division of your training sessions could look as follows

- Monday: recovery day
- Tuesday:
  - swimming: intensive
  - running: intensive
- Wednesday:
  - swimming: extensive training
  - cycling: extensive training
- Thursday
  - swimming: recovery training
  - running: recovery training
- Friday
  - cycling: intensive training
- Saturday
  - swimming: extensive training
  - cycling: long, easy endurance training (LSD)
- Sunday:
  - running: long, easy endurance training (LSD)

One day per week is preferably reserved as recovery day. If you are well trained this generally means a relative recovery day on which you train very quietly (one training session). If you are in less good shape you best opt for a recovery day on which you do not train at all.

week cycle

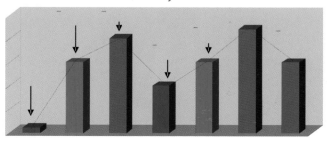

weeks

It is important to plan the training sessions, starting over a long period, and developing the plan more and more for the short term. You must know in advance where you want to go.

Nevertheless the plan should always show enough flexibility. There are always factors, such as weather conditions, illness, fatigue etc. that will disturb that planning. This means that planning cannot be entirely fixed, but that it will have to be continuously adjusted.

Chapter 7

Improving cycling

by correct nutrition

Two of the most important performance determining factors, besides your actual training, are your nutrition pattern and your fluid intake.

The cycling training of a triathlete is often very straining because often more than half of the total training time is spent on these cycling sessions. For this reason food and fluid intake before, during and after the cycling training sessions are vitally important.

To improve our insight into the importance of a good nutrition pattern we should ponder the energy supplies of the body.

The two large energy sources of the body are carbohydrates and fatty acids. In extreme circumstances, protein can also be applied as an energy source. In this last case, however, the muscles are literally demolished. It is clear that this would lead to a loss of condition within a very short period.

When are fatty acids and when are carbohydrates applied as energy source?

During very low intensity efforts, fatty acids are almost exclusively applied as your energy source. If the effort intensity increases, the share of carbohydrates will increase as an energy supplier, and during very intensive efforts, energy is exclusively provided by oxidation of carbohydrates. These carbohydrates have been piled up in the body under the form of glycogen in the muscles and in the liver. But this carbohydrate stock is limited. Generally it is believed that during very intense efforts the carbohydrate stock is consumed after approximately 90 minutes.

Research has shown that on average, after intensive training sessions, only 5% of the muscle glycogen consumed while training is replaced per hour. When muscle glycogen is completely exhausted, it takes 20 hrs before the muscle glycogen stocks again reach a normal level.

The fat stock in the body, on the other hand is seemingly inexhaustible. The disadvantage of drawing upon the energy supply by oxidation of fatty acids versus carbohydrates is that the fatty acids supply gets started more slowly, and less energy is provided by oxidation of fatty acids than by oxidation of carbohydrates, for the same quantity of oxygen intake.

Guidelines during and after low intensity cycling training sessions

When you train at low intensity, for example, during a very long and easy cycling training, fatty acids are consumed as an energy source. Especially when preparing for the long distance you will do a lot of training sessions at relatively low intensity. For all cycling training sessions which last longer than 3 hours you best use solid food that is lightly digestible. Energy-bars are very suitable to serve this purpose.

Since there is a sufficiently large stock of this energy source in the body, after the training sessions you can maintain a normal nutrition pattern, which consists on average of 60% carbohydrates, 25% fatty acids and 15% protein.

Supplementing fluid loss

For such long cycling training sessions it is essential that fluid loss is always sufficiently compensated, during and also after training. This loss of fluids (perspiration) has to do with the regulation of the body temperature. The vaporization of the sweat ensures the cooling of the body. This sweat vaporization is strongly influenced by temperature and humidity.

The body temperature rises much more rapidly in warm than in cool weather. Sweat evaporates quicker in warm and dry weather, and will cool the body more rapidly in these conditions than in warm and wet weather. This is particularly important for long-term efforts.

Abundant perspiration may have an important damaging impact on the body. Research has shown that a loss of just 1% leads to performance loss. A 3% to 5% loss can equal a fall of 10 to 30% of the performance capacity.

Why is that the case?

By reduction of the blood volume, blood becomes less liquid. Because of this, the heart will pump less effectively. Less oxygen can be transported to the working muscles and less sweat will be produced.

There will be less sweat vaporization, which will lead to the body temperature still increasing. Thus for endurance sportsmen like triathletes, the rectal temperature can rise in extreme cases to 40°C / 104°F and even still higher. A temperature of 41°C / 106°F is very dangerous and can cause irreparable damage to the liver, kidneys and brain.

Overheating can lead to the heat cramps, heat exhaustion and eventually heat collapse.

Cramps by heat generally occur in the calves when a person sweats exuberantly without compensating this loss.

Heat exhaustion is a further stage, and has the same cause. In this case activities must be immediately stopped.

Heat collapse is the most critical form of overheating and is not always preceded by cramps or exhaustion. Heat collapse blocks the thermoregulating mechanisms, and as a result, body temperature will strongly increase. A fast admission to a hospital is vital. First aid must ensure a fast cooling by water, ice or air.

It is wrong to think that overheating can only occur in endurance races in warm and wet weather. Long-term tough efforts in moderate climatological conditions can increase the body temperature drastically.

You must therefore, for long-term efforts in all weather conditions, keep paying attention to cooling and supplementing the fluid stocks!

Completing the fluid stock is best done by means of **water** or the so-called **thirst quencher**. A thirst quencher consists of water, a restricted quantity of carbohydrates and also minerals which compensate mineral loss from sweat secretion.

Research has shown that good general fitness gives the body a better resistance against heat. If you are well trained, you will   be better resistant against warm and wet conditions than when you are in less good shape.

TIPS for training sessions and races in warm conditions

- If possible you must acclimatize, meaning you must force up training during five to eight days progressively in a temperature in which the race will take place.
- Cool down your body by sprinkling it with water.
- Do your races and training sessions dressed lightly.
- Drink sufficiently during the race or training sessions This means approximately 10 to 15 cl fresh beverages each 15 min. Drinking more does not make much sense, because your body can only take in approximately 75 cl fluid per hour.

Guidelines for cycling training sessions with moderate intensity

Although the intensity already is a little bit higher, during these training sessions fatty acids are still used as the primary energy source. Depending on the training intensity, however, the share of carbohydrates used always increases. Replenishing the fluid lost by means of thirst quenchers is advisable here, to compensatefor the lost minerals and supplement the glycogen reserves. Beyond that, normal healthy nutrition should be sufficient.

Guidelines for cycling training sessions with high intensity

If you cycle to high intensity, for instance a threshold training session, carbohydrates are the primary source of energy.

It is best to have already replenished carbohydrates burned during training sessions lasting longer than one hour, in order to avoid an encounter with "the wall" or "the man with the hammer." The so-called **energy drinks** are very important here, because they allow replenishing carbohydrates burned in an easy manner during training or races. Of course you still need to use thirst quenchers as well to compensate the fluid loss.

Guidelines after an intensive cycling training session

After an intensive cycling training session or after a race, supplementing the carbohydrate stock is very important. You should start with this supplement within 30 minutes after training. Recent research has shown that maximal recovery can be reached by a combination of carbohydrates and protein, in a proportion of 50%-50%. Most **recovery drinks** meet these conditions.

Protein ensures that the negative nitrogen balance arisen from the intensive effort is neutralized. Preferably the first intake is liquid (recovery drink). Later you can switch to solid food, such as rice, pasta, bread etc. The share of the carbohydrates in solid nutrition can be now forced up to 70%.

Food having a high share of carbohydrates has a double function.

First, it leads to an increase of blood glucose as a result of which the exhausted muscles can be replenished.

Secondly, the body reacts to this increase of blood glucose with an insulin response to again decrease blood glucose. This insulin response is anabolic (muscle developing) because insulin stimulates the shaping of muscle protein.

Practically this means that you must start within 15 to 30 minutes after intensive training with the intake of 100g carbohydrates in combination with protein, followed by 100g carbohydrates every 2 hours following. It is advisable at the first and the second intake to use liquid carbohydrates (recovery drinks) because these are processed more rapidly than carbohydrates in solid form. Afterwards you can switch to food.

100 g carbohydrates are obtained from, for instance: 150 g muesli, 150 g raisins, 140 g spaghetti (raw), 350 g cooked rice, 500 g potatoes (cooked), 5 bananas, 200 g dried figs, 250 g whole-wheat bread.

Note

If carbohydrates must be taken in fast, you should choose products with a high **glycemic index** (GI). The GI is a measurement for the speed with which carbohydrates are incorporated into the blood and increase of blood sugar quality caused by this. Products having a high GI are, among other things, white bread, whole-wheat bread, cornflakes, muesli, bananas and raisins. Pastas only have an average GI.

When you do not complete your carbohydrate stock after intensive training sessions and races, your recovery goes slower. After some days of intensive training you feel spiritless and your training output decreases. It is clear that all this has a very negative impact on your final performance capacity.

The nutrition before the race

Some days before the race

During the days preceding an important and tough triathlon, the energy supply (carbohydrate stock) in the body can be intensified by means of adapting nutrition and training. Because of this, fatigue can be postponed during the race.

Practically speaking you operate as follows:
- train intensively up to 5 to 6 days before the race
- then gradually reduce the training quantity and quality (tapering)
- eat meals with a high share of carbohydrates during the last 3 days before the race

By following these directives muscle glycogen can exceed 20 to 40% above the normal level.

The day before the race a total of 600-800 g carbohydrates must be taken.

The day of the race

It is advisable having a meal with a high share of carbohydrates (150-200 g carbohydrates) 6 to 3 hours before the race. This way the food has been digested at the start of the race. Afterwards it is better not to   eat carbohydrates anymore, because too many carbohydrates in the blood could bring about an insulin reaction. Insulin is the hormone that keeps your carbohydrate stock in your blood on the right level. Due to this insulin reaction your sugar level may drop so much that you could feel tired and washed-out.

Carbohydrate intake just before the start of the race (5 to 10 minutes) causes no problem because these carbohydrates are only incorporated when the race has already started. During intense efforts there is no insulin reaction.

In warm and wet circumstances it can also be useful to build a fluid reserve. The cyclist can do this by drinking approximately 500ml water or thirst quencher during the last half hour before the race.

The nutrition during the race

Racing the Olympic distance

During an Olympic distance triathlon, carbohydrates are the most important energy source. When your carbohydrate stock is sufficiently filled, there is enough energy in the body for an intense effort lasting approximately 90 minutes. Since an Olympic distance triathlon lasts approximately 2 hours (and longer), the carbohydrate stock is a significant performance-determining factor. It is very important to replenish these energy stocks during the cycling component, in order to have all resources during the closing running component.

At the beginning of the cycling component, and afterwards each 15 minutes, use an energy drink which compensates the oxidation of carbohydrates. During cycling you should take in 40 to 60 grams of carbohydrates. If you have replenished your carbohydrates well during cycling, this is no longer necessary during the running component.

Especially in warm and wet weather conditions the fluid intake is enormously important. During the cycling component you should emphasize drinking energy drinks, as mentioned before. During the closing running component, water and thirst quenchers are most suitable.

Racing the Ironman distance

In long distance races, energy is provided by the oxidation of fatty acids and carbohydrates. Fatty acids do not have to be completed, because the stock in the body is more than enough.

During the swimming component you have already burned a part of your carbohydrates, and therefore it is very important to replenish this stock as soon as possible, starting at the beginning of the cycling component.

During the first half of the cycling component you can do this by eating solid food, such as sandwiches and energy bars. What you eat must be precisely tested during your long cycling training sessions! You would best advised to test lightly digestible products with a high caloric value.

During cycling you must drink a lot. Per hour you should take at least 0.5 to 0.75 liters (in warm weather). This amounts during the cycling component of an Ironman distance race to a total of 4 liters! More is useless, because your body cannot process a larger quantity. Vary water and energy drinks. Possibly you can, for the change in taste, compose a drink yourself. There are triathletes who mix Coca Cola with water (proportion 1-1). Make sure that the gas has disappeared from the coke by preparing the drink the day before, by shaking thoroughly and afterwards leave the bottles with the mixture open overnight!

Guidelines for healthy nutrition

As mentioned before, the nutrition of a triathlete must comprise 60% carbohydrates (during intensive training days and stage races even up to 70%), 20-25% fats and 15% protein.

Generally speaking, the following products are advisable: lots of vegetables, preferably uncooked; a lot of fruit; pasta, rice, potatoes, brown bread; chicken and fish; skimmed and semi-skimmed dairy products; muesli and other cereals.

The following products are not recommended: fat meat products; fried food; whole dairy products; salt; excessive sweets (cakes, cookies, chocolate...); alcohol; crisps; ....

Furthermore, you must pay much attention to the fluid intake during the day. This means that during the day you must regularly drink water apart from training. Water is preferred to coffee, because coffee has a water secreting impact. The use of coffee must be therefore limited. Moreover, coffee blocks the intake of Vit.C.

Must fats be absolutely avoided?

Your nutrition is built around the intake of carbohydrates. This does not mean, however, that fats must be avoided systematically. On the contrary, if you train intensely and regularly you should not be afraid to consciously eat fats at regular times. Fats ensure, by means of LDL-cholesterol, the production of the steroids, among which is the anabolic hormone testosterone. A light body weight and little bodily fat are connected in several studies with men having a very low testosterone quality. This already rapidly results in a slowed down recovery from training labor.

Although saturated fats cannot be avoided completely, unsaturated fats must be preferred. These are, among other things, found in vegetable oil, nuts, seeds and fat fish.

6% body fat

Over the last years the fixed idea has arisen that a triathlete only stands sharp if his body fat is reduced to 6%. This is absolutely untrue, because the percentage body fat is very personal. Some athletes have by nature a very low percentage body fat. For them it is not difficult to reach 6%. Other athletes have, by nature, a much higher percentage of body fat. They reach that 6% only after following a very strict diet, in which they always show a negative energy balance. They take in too few carbohydrates, as a result of which the energy stocks in their muscles are no longer replenished after intense training. Also, in the nutrition pattern of these athletes there is generally no room for fats. The consequence often is a spectacular drop in their performance potential. Research has shown that excessively fast weight loss leads to reduction of the aerobic and anaerobic capacity, of absolute strength and of strength endurance.

Therefore following a very strict diet is for most athletes catastrophic.

The ideal weight of a triathlete cannot be captured in a postulated weight or fat percentage. You know from experience when you are "sharp," and which weight you must reach to achieve your best performances. If you train well, and take into account the elementary nutrition directives mentioned above, strict diets are not necessary.

Do protein supplements have to be taken?

In contrast to the intake of carbohydrates, you can assume that a normal nutrition pattern always contains sufficient protein.

An endurance sportsman has a daily protein need of approximately 1.3 g/kilogram. An athlete weighing 70 kilograms needs approximately 91 g protein per day. If you know that a piece of chicken weighing approximately 200 g already provides almost half of the daily amount, it should be clear that you do not have to strive for extra protein supplementing. Besides the necessary protein intake (combined with carbohydrates) right after an intense training session or after a race, (slight) supplementing can be considered only at the beginning of a new training set-up.

Protein is the building material of the body. Protein is called upon as an energy source of the body in extreme cases, viz. at complete and continuing exhaustion of the glycogen stocks.

Share of Kcal, protein, fats and carbohydrates of some common nutrients by 100 g

	Kcal	Protein	Fat	Carbohydrates
Banana	88	1	0	20
Apple	50	0	0	12
Orange	47	1	0	11
Kiwi	40	1	0	9
Muesli without sugar	390	11	8	68
Muesli with sugar	396	11	11	64
Oat malt	363	13	7	62
Cornflakes	370	7	1	84
Muesli bar	440	5	17	67
Milk skimmed	37	4	0.1	5
Milk semi-skimmed	46	4	1.5	5
Milk whole	63	4	3.4	5
Yoghourt skimmed	35	4	0.1	4
Yoghourt semi-skimmed	49	4	1.5	5
Yoghourt whole	85	5	4.5	6
Brown bread	248	10	3	45
Whole-wheat bread	222	9	3	41
Margarine	730	0	80	1

	Kcal	Protein	Fat	Carbohydrates
Cheese 20 +	245	34	12	0
Cheese 50 +	370	23	31	0
Ham, raw	199	23	12	0
Chicken roll	166	24	7	2
Chocolate sprinklings	431	6	17	64
Marmalade	112	0	0	28
Spaghetti raw	350	12	2	71
Spaghetti cooked	94	3	1	19
Pizza, cheese and tomato				
Rice unboiled	346	7	1	78
Rice cooked	147	3	0	33
Potato, cooked	76	2	0	17
Fries	310	5	15	38
cauliflower, raw	14	2	0	2
Carrots, raw	11	1	0	2
Endive, raw	5	1	0	0
Peas, cooked	60	4	0	11
Raw vegetables	14	1	0	2
Tomatoes	11	1	0	2
Leek, raw	24	1	0	0
Vegetable soup	34	1	2	3
Cod fish, cooked	105	23	1	0
Salmon	271	28	18	0
Chicken filet	158	31	4	0

	Kcal	Protein	Fat	Carbohydrates
Turkey filet	158	31	4	0
Breakfast bacon	404	15	38	0
Pork tenderloin	147	28	4	0
Beefsteak	139	27	3	1
Roast beef	167	28	6	1
Pudding, vanilla	114	4	3	19
Ice	182	3	9	22

What to do in case of overweight?

A lot of triathletes struggle with overweight during, and even after, the relative recovery period. They had to restrain from too many things during the race period, and therefore slacken the reins too much at a certain point. Sometimes it is very difficult to lose weight again.

Following a strict diet during a longer period is being strictly dissuaded.

An excessive negative energy balance (more energy is consumed than is taken in) leads after some time to reduction of the muscles (protein is used as energy supplier), prevents the recovery of the body and therefore leads to overtraining, bringing along a significant fall of the performance potential.

TIPS against being overweight

- Limit weight increase during the winter period. It makes no sense to eat without brakes during the preparation period. Stop at 2 to 3 kilograms above the ideal weight.

- When overweight, start early with an adapted nutrition pattern, avoiding useless nutrition such as sweets and soda. If necessary you should strive for a slightly negative energy balance, so that the ideal weight can be reached very gradually. This slightly negative energy balance is only necessary when, in spite of the adapted nutrition pattern and increasing training labor, the body weight does not decrease. Maximum 2 kilograms per month seems a rate of weight loss.

- It is best for a triathlete to lose weight by means of long, easy endurance training sessions. During these training sessions fats are oxidized. Intensive training sessions mainly oxidize carbohydrates.

- When following a diet you must always pay enough attention to the fact that the diet is not at the expense of carbohydrates. Especially intensive training labor requires permanently replenishing the carbohydrates under all circumstances. For reasons mentioned above, fat must keep its place in nutrition as well.

How about nutrition supplements and other preparations?

Concerning nutrition supplements and preparations, it is difficult to still see the forest for the trees.

Some supplements, however, prove to be supportive of your training labor:

- **Arginine and ornitine:**
  - amino acids which, when administered in sufficiently large quantities, stimulate the pituitary gland. Because of this, the production of the human growth hormone is stimulated. The growth hormone improves recovery after effort.

- **Glutamine:**
  - an amino acid which reduces muscle demolition and reinforces the immune system.

- **Antioxidants:**
  - in the body, as a result of the metabolism and energy production, free radicals are being produced. These free radicals are, among other things, responsible for cardiac diseases, some forms of cancers, ageing and muscular aches after effort. Research has also shown that training increases the amount of free radicals.

    Antioxidants are substances which neutralize the damaging effect of free radicals. Thus the damage to muscle cells would be less for sportsmen who take supplementing antioxidants than for those who do not take these supplements.

- **Vitamins and mineral supplements:**
  - quite a lot of athletes take such supplements, and generally even in very large quantities. These supplements are necessary, since too little fruit and vegetables are eaten. A cyclist who eats 4 to 6 pieces of fruit every day, and also eats fresh vegetables, does not need these (expensive) preparations.

- **Vitamin C:**
  - this vitamin deserves particular attention. On the one hand it belongs to the antioxidants, on the other hand it has been proven that vitamin C raises the resistance of the body against infections.

  A triathlete who trains intensely has an inferior resistance against infections, because the straining effort has decreased the resistance against these infections. Vitamin C raises this resistance to a sufficiently high level. One to two grams/day during periods of intense training and races seems suitable. When infections arise some doctors even prescribe five grams/day.

- **Iron:**
  - iron supplement is only necessary if there is an iron shortage, i.e., too low ferritine quality. Many athletes systematically take iron preparations, even without a shortage being established. This makes no sense, since it can be dangerous to your health because the iron surplusis piled up in the spinal cord and in organs such as the liver.

General conclusion

1. Always drink sufficiently, even in cooler weather – if possible during training sessions, but certainly immediately after.

2. Replenish the energy stocks during intensive training sessions and races, preferably by means of energy drinks. Per hour 60-70 g carbohydrates must be consumed.

3. Always replenish energy stocks after the intensive training sessions and races. Within 15 to 30 minutes after the training session/race, start using recovery drinks, having a proportion of 50% carbohydrates and 50% protein.

4. After using the energy drinks, the muscles must be reactivated by means of meals having a high share of carbohydrates (bread, rice, pasta, potatoes).

5. Adjust the nutrition pattern as a function of training labor. The energy intake during recovery days must be significantly lower than during intensive training days or race days.

6. The nutrition products having a high share of carbohydrates have to be the main part of the whole nutrition composition.

7. Make sure that fat still accounts for 20% of the total nutrition pattern. It is wrong to systematically ban it from nutrition.

8. Consciously limit the weight increase during the relative rest period.

9. Gradually scale back the body weight to the ideal weight when overweight.

10. Never economize on the intake of carbohydrates during a diet.

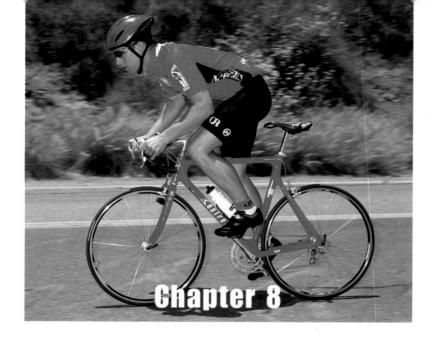

Chapter 8

Overtraining

and tips to prevent overtraining

What is overtraining?

Triathlon is a passion, and is literally addictive. Quite soon you will compare distances and times, with yourself and in comparison with others. How long? How far? Quicker and further. You always want more. Cycling is for a lot of triathletes the ideal means to attain a large overall training volume. For a lot of triathletes, 20 hours training per week is often an objective. But is all this effective?

You may feel you have trained well and exstensively, but your results stagnate and later slacken. Often this prompts you to train even harder, devouring still more kilometers without any improvement. On the contrary, performances will often decline even further. How is that possible?

To answer this question we need to analyze the term **training**.

Training is administering systematic physical stimulations to the body, taking into account the capacity of the body. These stimulations bring about changes in the body which lead, when considering the correct proportion of effort and recovery, to an increase of the performance capacity.

In this definition there are some important data:

- **Taking into account the capacity of the body:**
  Every triathlete has a certain training capacity. This capacity can vary from one day to the next. Insufficient sleep, bad nutrition, illness, stress can all reduce the capacity of the body.

Not every triathlete has the same capacity. Some triathletes can perform more training labor than others. Triathlon is indeed a very straining sport. Therefore it makes no sense to just copy training set-ups of good triathletes.

It is far more important to take into account the training principles applied by good triathletes, and apply these principles considering your own capacity. Moreover it is not so that the triathlete with the largest capacity by definition also obtain the best results. Some athletes can achieve better results with a lower training tax than athletes who train harder and more frequently.

Overtraining arises if the training stimuli are stronger than the individual capacity. It is possible to distinguish *qualitative overtraining* and *quantitative overtraining*.

The cause for **qualitative overtraining** is typically found in the intensity of the training pivots, i.e. you train too intensively. In **quantitative overtraining**, on the other hand, the training volume is too large – the training duration is too long. Overtraining often appears as a combination of these two forms.

Therefore it is very important that training intensity and training volume are forced up gradually. In the beginning of a training set-up you should first of all pay attention to gradually forcing up training volume. In other words you must always strive for a large basic endurance (aerobic endurance) before starting to train more intensively.

You constantly have to give your body opportunity to adapt to the rising training workload. Intensifying the training workload too suddenly, qualitatively or quantitatively, leads to a drop in performance level after a while.

At that moment you are very liable to overload injuries. Especially a new training set-up, after a period of obliged inactivity or after a tough race period, should be handled with care. Even for the best-trained triathletes there is a shaky balance between performance improvement and overtraining.

- **Considering the correct proportion effort – recovery:**
  It may sound strange, but training itself decreases the performance level. By the end of the training session you are tired and unable to repeat the session. A positive training impact is possible only after a sufficiently long recovery period. This mechanism is called the **principle of supercompensation**.

The principle of supercompensation

The principle of supercompensation is the most important training principle for a triathlete, but at the same time it also is the most difficult to apply.

According to this principle, the training impact can only be obtained when training is followed by a sufficiently long recovery period.

This seems very logical, but for a triathlete who has to train for three different disciplines, the application of this principle is far from simple. The next diagram explains this principle:

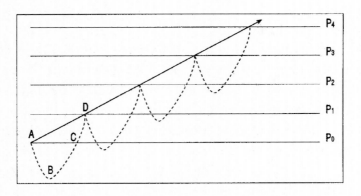

P0, P1, P2, P3, P4... different performance levels
AB: drop of the performance level as a result of training fatigue
BC: rise of the performance level during recovery period
CD: the **supercompensation***. As a result of the training labor the performance level of the triathlete mounted to a higher level.*

We see that optimum training impact can only be obtained if the next training stimulation is given, and the top of supercompensation has been reached.

As a triathlete you are faced with a number of fundamental questions:
- When have you fully recovered to start training again (in other words how much time do you need to reach supercompensation after a certain training session)?

- How intense can this next training session be?

- What is the influence of the training for other disciplines (swimming and running) on the time needed to reach supercompensation after a cycling training session?

The time to reach supercompensation is determined by a number of elements
- *Your degree of training:*
  You will recover sooner if you are well trained.

- *The nature of the training session:*
  The more intense the training session is, the longer recovery phase lasts. Slow endurance cycling training demands significantly less recovery time than intensive interval cycling training.

- *Training sessions done during the recovery phase of your cycling training*
  An endurance training session for swimming is less straining after an intensive cycling training session than a long endurance run.

- *Correct nutrition*
  Being a triathlete, you demand a lot from your body. You train several hours a day, which consumes a lot of energy. The correct nutrition in combination with thirst quenchers, energy and recovery drinks (see elsewhere) is essential for an optimal recovery phase.

- *Your mental state:*
  There is a clear link between your mental state and your recovery time after training. If you are mentally stressed for whatever reason, you will recuperate slower from efforts (thus you need more time to reach supercompensation) in comparison to when being relaxed.

- *A normal sleep pattern:*
  A normal sleep pattern is also important. Because of a series of hormonal processes it is important to go to bed at a normal time and to get up early. The testosterone quality in blood undergoes an increase during the night, to reach a peak in the morning.

  The human growth hormone, which is, among other things, responsible for the recovery of the body after intense efforts, reaches maximal values during the night. A good night's rest optimizes the functioning of these hormones.

- *Blood analysis on a regular base*
  Due to frequent and demanding training sessions it is possible that certain shortages arise in the blood. After blood analysis, possible shortages (e.g. Fe, B12 etc.) can be discovered in time and afterwards be completed.

Indications in order to determine the top of supercompensation:

- *Your subjective feeling:*
  If you feel tired, you will certainly not have reached the top of supercompensation yet. There is of course "normal" fatigue after a rough training session. Sometimes fatigue lingers, even after a normal night's rest, and your legs feel sluggish and even painful while cycling. Continuing to complete your training set-up under these circumstances does not make sense. You must always keep in mind that a tired body is not trainable; on the contrary you can only obtain a reverse effect by training. Triathletes are most of the time very passionate, and therefore it is often hard to admit you feel tired.

- *Blood analyses:*
  By means of a series of parameters, such as the number of red blood cells, hemoglobin quality, the haematocrit value (the proportion of the number of red blood cells to the total plasma volume) etc., doctors can establish whether or not you are wearing yourself out by means of training. Such analyses are however rather expensive and can only be carried out a few times per year.

- *Submaximal or maximal tests:*
  The performance level during these tests, paired with other parameters such as the curve of the heart rate during the test, can offer an idea of the recovery process.

- *The registration of the heart rate during training:*
  If you are used to training and using a heart rate monitor, you can observe quite quickly whether your

training heart rate corresponds to the normal heart rate paired with the effort made.

If you realize that your heart rate is higher than usual, this can be an indication that you have not yet recuperated sufficiently from the preceding training session. It is however also possible that a low heart rate, the feeling that you cannot increase the heart rate, indicates fatigue (see further).

• *A clear insight in the nature of the training sessions undertaken*
It is advisable to keep a training diary. You are well aware of the type of training you have done and you can adjust, in case of fatigue, your recovery phase.

The next table shows the recovery time needed as a function of the nature of the training session.

Recovery time after different types of training intensity

Recovery time ↓ Type of work load →	aërobic	85-95% Aërobic-anaërobic	95-100% Anaërobic	strength
During the effort	Intensity 60-70%			
Immediate but incomplete recovery		After 1.5 to 2 h	After 2 h	After 2 h
90-95% recovery	At intensity 75-80% after 12 h	After 12 h	After 12 to 18 h	After 18 h
Complete recovery	At intensity 75-80% after 24 to 36 h	After 24 to 48 h	After 48 to 72 h	After 72 to 84 h

From this table you can deduce, among other things, that you have to wait after an intensive training session at least 3 days before you may do the same training tax once again.

All this does not mean that you cannot train during the recovery phase after intensive training. After a very intensive training session (with repeated efforts at an anaerobic level) recovery training is, in the first place, advisable. After a more moderate intensive session (training sessions around threshold), calm long endurance training of another discipline can be undertaken without any problems occurring. This training session must then again be followed by recovery training.

- The recording of resting heart rate (see before).
  All the previous shows that your training labor is only effective sufficient (relative) recovery time is inserted after training to reach supercompensation.

What happens if the recovery time after training has not been sufficient becomes clear from the next diagram:

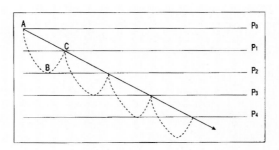

P0, P1, P2, P3, P4... different performance levels
AB: drop of the performance level as a result of training fatigue
BC: the rise of the performance level during recovery period is insufficient as a result of insufficient recovery time. A new training stimulus was inserted too early. As a result of this there is no supercompensation, and we see a drop instead of a rise of the performance level.

Other causes of overtraining

You must learn to listen to your body. Painful and rigid muscles, a general feeling of fatigue, a stagnation or fall of the performance level, a raised morning pulse often are indications that the training intensity (quantitatively and/or qualitatively) is too high. Drastically diminishing the training quantity or even complete rest is recommended to avoid getting into the traditional ailing dead end from which there is no escape.

It is not always easy to even scale back training. You are soon afraid that months of training labor is lost if you do less or no training for some days.

The causes of overtraining are often situated outside training
- *Successive races without sufficient chance of recovery*

- *Stress, mental difficulties*
  Relationship problems, etc. reduce the individual capacity. In a training plan you need to take into account "difficult periods," during which you cannot train as much.

- *Insufficient sleep*
  It is vitally important to sleep sufficiently. A good night's rest is essential, and even a short nap after a straining training session can have a positive effect.

- *Infection, such as influenza*
  Just like when fatigued, an important principle should be applied here: a sick body is never, under absolutely no circumstances, trainable. It is often difficult to interrupt training. You are afraid that training labor will

be lost. It does not make any sense to train when sick, and it is even dangerous. Absolute rest accelerates the healing process. Training when ill can leave long-term marks. Unfortunately here and there the idea still exists of "sweating out" influenza. This idea is not only absurd, but it can even be life-threatening.

- *Unbalanced diet*
  The nutrition pattern of a triathlete who trains several hours daily must be well figured out as a function of these efforts. Especially the share of the carbohydrates in nutrition is very important.

- *A negative energy balance*
  This means that more energy is consumed than taken in. This often occurs when striving for an (unrealistic) ideal weight and following a low-carb diet to reach this weight.

- *Dehydration*
  The fluid lost by perspiration must be replenished both during and after training. The idea of dressing "thick" during training, and this way reach ideal weight by means of perspiration, has very disadvantageous consequences on the performance level.

- *Heat*
  Warm and wet weather conditions decrease your capacity and performance potential. It is thus advisable to reduce the training workload in abnormally warm weather conditions.

- *Using medication*
  If you take medicines, you must always consult your doctor to know which impact these medicines will have

on your capacity and whether or not they have a negative impact when practicing a sport intensely.

- *Jetlag*
  It is a general belief that the time needed to adapt to a time zone change amounts to one hour per day time difference. When traveling long distances and undergoing the accompanying time difference, it is advisable to train very calmly during the first days.

Recognizing overtraining

To avoid overtraining it is not only necessary to know the causes of overtraining, but also to have insight into the symptoms.

An important symptom of overtraining is a decrease of the maximum performance capacity. You'll also notice that your heart rate increases less rapidly than usual during effort, and that you have to put in more effort than normal to increase your heart rate to a certain level. Often this is preceded by a period in which your resting heart rate also has increased. Recovery after effort is slowed down, although in some cases, in spite of overtraining, the heart rate rapidly drops after effort.

Furthermore there are still a number of mental indications of overtraining. You do not feel like training, you are irritable, you are not very hungry and you sleep less well. In addition you have a raised chance of infections.

A specific example of the raised risk on infections is herpes. Herpes is a viral infection which often appears as cysts (also called fever cysts) on the lip or around the mouth. Once contaminated by it, the virus that causes herpes is always latently present in the body. During periods of reduced capacitance, for example, when training (too) much, this infection breaks through.

You also notice that you are more susceptible to colds during periods of heavy training, or when you are in good shape. Colds are the consequence of contact with certain viruses. If the defense system against these viruses is weak, the odds of catching a cold increase. Research has proven that intensive training weakens the defense system. Hence athletes in top condition, after they have trained intensely, are more subject to these viruses.

Recognizing overtraining is often difficult, because a low heart rate during the effort, or a fast recovery of the heart rate after the effort can be interpreted as positive training impact. Moreover during a lactic acid test used when there is possible overtraining, a reduced lactic acid quality during effort is established. This can also lead to misinterpretation.

To recognize overtraining much attention must be paid to your mental state. Do you feel good, are you eager to train, do you have a normal sleeping pattern and a normal appetite, and do you process training smoothly? When you start to feel like you are in a training rut, it is advisable to stop training or scale back. A lot of scientists are convinced that overtraining is largely a mental issue. For this reason, variation in training, and disruptions in training during which you look for entertainment not involving your sport, are necessary.

It is also important to examine if your heart rate obtains normal values during training. The heart rate which does not increase easily during training and therefore remains abnormally low in spite of increasing strain is often a sign that you are tired. It is best to again plan a recovery period.

In spite of all the previous observations, you cannot lose sight of the fact that you can be tired during a training session and a race without this implying overtraining. Before you can obtain positive training impact, you should have been tired. It is, however, important that you insert sufficient recovery after efforts in order to reach supercompensation.

You should also distinguish overload from overtraining: In case of overload, fatigue disappears after a few days, and you will perform better after some days of recovery.

In case of overtraining, fatigue keeps on bugging you, even after some recovery days. Your performance level remains reduced.

How can you prevent overtraining?

Determining overtraining is not simple, because at first sight you generally connect a reduction of the performance level with too little training than with too much training. Really determining overtraining often happens late. The consequence is that you keep trying to catch up with the facts. It is also difficult to determine the cause of overtraining. For this reason there are a number of means to help you.

Keeping a training diary

In the training diary, the following issues are noted day after day: precise description of the kind of training done: duration, distance, intensity; How was training experienced (easy, tough...); How does recovery go? Registration of the resting heart rate; Weight; Mental state; possibly other observations.

When there are symptoms of overtraining, you can consult the training diary and look for the beginning of the overtraining and possible causes.

Filling in a questionnaire

By filling in a questionnaire daily the risk of overtraining can be visualized:

QUESTIONNAIRE OVERTRAINING

Date:...........

Item	score		
Training	1	2	3
Resting heart rate	1	2	3
Health	1	2	3
Sleep	1	2	3
Nutrition	1	2	3
Social	1	2	3
Stress	1	2	3

Total ....

Explanation:

1 = excellent
2 = average, could be better
3 = bad

Training:
1 = training goes optimally, feeling good while training
2 = training does not go really smoothly
3 = training is experienced as too tough, the recovery does not go well

Resting heart rate:
1 = normal morning pulse
2 = morning pulse more than 10% higher than usual
3 = morning pulse more than 15% higher than usual

Health:
1 = feeling good, fit, healthy
2 = not 100% fit, not feeling good overall
3 = feeling bad, sick (never train)

Sleep:
1 = excellent sleep
2 = sleep could be better
3 = disturbed sleep, often awake, still tired in the morning

Nutrition:
1 = appetite is alright
2 = appetite is not optimal
3 = no appetite or strict diet

Social:	1 = everything alright with relationships (at home, school, boyfriend, girlfriend, work.)
	2 = social contacts not optimal
	3 = relationship problems
Stress:	1 = feeling relaxed
	2 = slightly stressed
	3 = stressed, irritable, hot under the collar

For every item, the score is indicated daily and the total is made. When scoring 1 for every item you obtain on that day you will get a total of 7. The total score fluctuates between minimum 7 and maximum 21. Total of every daily score is presented in a graph.

If you see a rising line in the curve of the daily scores, the danger of overtraining exists. Then you can make an analysis of the causes of the increase of the curve and you can intervene before overtraining manifests itself.

Risk for overtraining

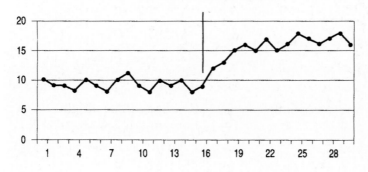

Tips to prevent overtraining
- Insert a day of rest or a relative recovery day when feeling tired
- Always try to get a good night's rest
- Take into account reduced resistance of the body in periods of stress, abnormally tough weather condtions etc.
- Always make sure there is sufficient carbohydrate intake during and after intensive training sessions and races
- Always make sure there is enough fluid intake during and after training sessions and races, even when it is not really wet and warm
- An intensive training day should always be followed by a day training extensively or by a (relative) recovery day
- Daily, fill in a training diary and/or fill in the overtraining questionnaire
- Scale back the training sessions sufficiently when preparing an important race
- Pay attention to all possible symptoms of overtraining

Impact of Detraining

Permanent training impact only is realized and preserved when training is sufficiently intensive, and the training program shows sufficient regularity and is systematic.

As mentioned before, the most important effects of endurance training are:
- An increase of the maximal oxygen intake (VO_2max)
  Research has shown that moderate endurance training raises VO_2max by 10 to 20%, and thorough and long-term endurance training can lead to an increase of up to 25% of VO_2max.

- An increase of the stroke volume. This means that the quantity of blood which is expelled by each heart beat increases, allowing more oxygen per heart rate to be transported to the active muscles.

- An increase in the number or capillaries surrounding individual muscle fibers. Because of this the delivery of oxygen and nutrients to the muscles, the removal or metabolic waste products rises. The increase of the number of capillaries can amount up to 50% above the values of untrained people.

What happens if training is interrupted?
- If training is interrupted entirely, one notices that especially during the first month a strong drop of VO_2max appears, followed by a further, but slower fall during the following two months. The level of the VO_2max nevertheless is still higher than the level of untrained people. A (limited) positive impact remains, even after 3 months of "detraining."

- The fall of the stroke volume follows the same curve

- The increased capillary density, on the other hand, proves to have remained the same for well-trained endurance athletes after 3 months of detraining. For less well trained athletes, a substantial fall may be determined.

We notice that completely interrupting training has a strongly opposite impact: in a few weeks' time, much of a laboriously built condition is lost. Your condition, for which you perhaps have worked for years, disappears much more rapidly than the amount of time it took to build it.

It is nevertheless the case that you need significantly less time to again reach a certain condition, than the time which you needed to initially reach that level.

After 10 days of detraining, it will require more than 10 days to return to the initial trained level. It will take more or less 30 days to get back to the level you had at the beginning of your detraining.

Twenty days of detraining requires, theoretically speaking, 40 days to return to your initial level.

Studies have, however, proven that a duration sportsman can preserve his condition during 20 weeks when training labor is reduced by 40%, keeping the intensity relatively identical.
Therefore you should not be afraid to lose your condition if you train a little less.

Chapter 9

Other performance determining factors

Your eventual performance level is not only determined by your training, but also by a number of other factors.

Medical support

Although you should not exaggerate, restricted medical support is a must, since the training sessions demand much from the body.

Blood analysis

Regular blood control can be established if the triathlete has certain shortages and if training possibly needs to be adjusted.

Some important blood parameters which influence the performances directly or indirectly are:

- **The red blood cells (RBC):**
  The RBC take care of the transport of oxygen in the body. A high number of RBC is therefore favorable for a triathlete. Experience teaches that after a period of tough training sessions or races, the number of RBC often decreases. After a recovery period, an increase could be determined. A fall in number of RBC can be an indication to scale back the training volume.

- Hemoglobin:
  Hemoglobin is a protein which links itself with oxygen. A high hemoglobin quality is therefore interesting for a triathlete because his oxygen transport rises. This quality also seems related to (too) tough training labor.

- The hematocrit:
  This is the proportion of the number of RBC with respect to the total blood volume. For this reason high hematocrit value indicates a high oxygen transport capacity, and this is very interesting for a triathlete.

- Creatinkinase (CK):
  CK is an enzyme that indicates muscle reduction. Too intensive training sessions or insufficient recovery between the training sessions and/or races lead to a high CK-value. High CK-value is an absolute indication to reduce the training intensity.

- **Urea:**
  Urea is a substance which is released when proteins are demolished. A too high urea quality in sportsmen can indicate that too little fluid is taken in during and after the training sessions.

- **Testosterone:**
  Testosterone is an anabolic (constructive) hormone. A fall in testosterone quality can indicate that the body no longer processes training. Reducing the training strain, both quantitatively and qualitatively is strongly advisable in this case.

- **Cortisol:**
  Cortisol is a catabolic (demolishing) hormone. An increase of cortisol quality indicates that training is no longer processed well. The proportion of testosterone to cortisol is also important. Fall of testosterone quality and simultaneous increase of the cortisol quality is an indication that the triathlete recuperates insufficiently.

- **Vitamin B12 and folium acid:**
  Vitamin B12 and folium acid are needed to build proteins and RBC.

- **Ferritine:**
  Ferritine is a protein iron complex which indicates the iron reserve in the body. Iron is needed for the production of RBC and hemoglobin. A shortage of iron decreases hemoglobin quality and the number of RBC.

- **Magnesium:**
  Magnesium is an important factor in energy metabolism and influences the nerve muscle sensitivity.

Shortage of magnesium manifests itself clinically by a disturbed nerve muscle function (among other things cramps) and muscle weakness.

Altitude training

The parameters above show that the number of red blood cells is an important element in the performance capacity of the triathlete.

A natural means to multiply this number is altitude training. On a certain altitude the body adapts to the reduced atmospheric pressure by producing new red blood cells.

The conditions for good altitude training are: stay at an altitude of more than 1500m for at least 3 weeks.

In practice an altitude training period must be subdivided into a number of phases:
- Phase 1: the acclimatization phase (3 to 5 days)
  You should give your body time to adapt to the altitude. On average this phase lasts 3 days. In the beginning of this phase there is a clearly raised resting heart rate. Your normal training volume must be consciously scaled back until your resting heart rate has reached its normal value.
- Phase 2: (5 days)
  Training volume is progressively intensified. You only do less intensive training sessions.
- Phase 3:
  During the previous phases the body has gotten time to adapt optimally to altitude. This also means that the training intensity can be forced up. Do not forget, however, that the body recovers more slowly from efforts made. You should pay enough attention to the recovery phase after training.

What do you have to take into account when returning to sea level?
The first 10 days after returning to sea level are necessary to adapt again to the new situation. During this phase the emphasis is on lighter, extensive training sessions. This phase is a supercompensation phase to maximally profit from the effects of the past altitude training. After these 10 days you reach a stage of increased performance level. Especially the period between day 14 and 21 would be ideal to achieve top performances.

But not all studies unequivocally emphasize the positive impact of altitude training, because

- The maximum heart rate decreases by 1% for each 400m altitude
- The maximum oxygen intake capacity decreases by 10% for each 1000m, starting to count from 1200m
- To reach the same performance as on sea level, more carbohydrates are consumed at altitude
- Speed with which lactic acid is removed has slowed down
- When training at altitude, recovery has slowed down
- By the fall of the plasma volume, the increase of the number of RBC and hemoglobin is only relative
- The quality of the RBC has decreased
- Generally speaking the athlete sleeps less well during an altitude training period
- The appetite diminishes in comparison with sea level
- At altitude there is a higher risk of dehydration

Sometimes you can opt for other procedures to get around these disadvantages, namely training at altitude and sleeping at sea level, or training at sea level and sleeping at altitude.

Especially this last procedure is said to be most effective. The research results on this are however not certified.

Photo & Illustration Credits

Graphics: Paul Van Den Bosch

Photos: Polar Electro Belgium nv
                 Pieter Desmedt-Jans
                 Octagon NV
                 Bakke/Svensson/WTC

Model for the strength exercises and stretching photos:
                 Peter Croes

Cover Design: Jens Vogelsang

Cover Photo: dpa picture-alliance, Germany

IRONMAN EDITION

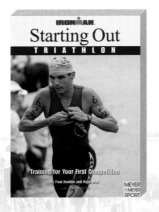
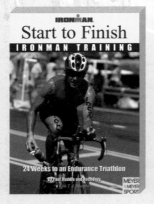
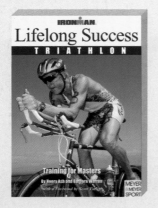

OFFICIAL IRONMAN BOOKS

Ironman Edition
Ash/Warren
Lifelong Training
Advanced Training for Masters

272 pages, full-color print
52 photos, numerous illustrations
and tables
Paperback, $5^{3}/4$" x $8^{1}/4$"
ISBN: 1-84126-104-1
£ 14.95 UK/$ 19.95 US
$ 29.95 CDN/€ 18.90

Ironman Edition
Sheila Dean
Nutrition & Endurance
Where Do I Begin?

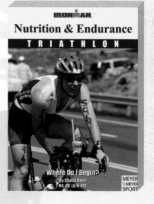

144 pages, full-color print
36 photos, 10 tables
Paperback, $5^{3}/4$" x $8^{1}/4$"
ISBN: 1-84126-105-X
£ 12.95 UK/$ 17.95 US
$ 25.95 CDN/€ 16.90

Ironman Edition
T. J. Murphy
The Unbreakable Athlete
Injury Prevention

152 pages, full-color print
52 photos
Paperback, $5^{3}/4$" x $8^{1}/4$"
ISBN: 1-84126-109-2
£ 12.95 UK/$ 17.95 US
$ 25.95 CDN/€ 16.95

MEYER & MEYER Sport | sales@m-m-sports.com | www.m-m-sports.com

MEYER
& MEYER
SPORT